Tamerlane's Children

Robert Rand is a journalist, independent radio producer, and editor. For three years he was based in Tashkent working as a writer and freelance journalist, and his radio pieces about Uzbekistan were aired on National Public Radio and Public Radio International. He has also written for *The New Yorker*, and is the author of several books, including *Comrade Lawyer: Inside Soviet Justice in an Era of Reform*, *My Suburban Shtetl* and *Dancing Away an Anxious Mind*. He lives in Tarrytown, New York.

Tamerlane's Children

Dispatches from Contemporary Uzbekistan

Robert Rand

ONEWORLD
OXFORD

Oneworld Publications
(Sales and editorial)
185 Banbury Road
Oxford OX2 7AR
England
www.oneworld-publications.com

© Robert Rand 2006

All rights reserved.
Copyright under Berne Convention.
A CIP record for this title is available
from the British Library.

ISBN-13: 978–1–85168–457–1
ISBN-10: 1–85168–457–3

Typeset by Jayvee, India
Cover design by Liz Powell
Printed and bound in India for Imprint Digital

Learn more about Oneworld. Join our mailing list to
find out about our latest titles and special offers at:

www.oneworld-publications.com/newsletter.htm

For Katrina

Contents

Introduction

From August 2001 to November 2004, I lived and worked in Uzbekistan. I went there essentially as a trailing spouse: my wife is a United Nations employee, and she had the opportunity to take a position in Tashkent, the Uzbek capital. I had made a career as a journalist and writer, spoke Russian and was deeply interested in the former Soviet Union, so I valued the chance to experience Central Asia, and Uzbekistan in particular, the region's most populous country. So off we went, with our two-year-old son in tow.

Three-and-a-half years later we returned to our home in New York. A daughter had been added to our family. And Oneworld most generously committed to publish *Tamerlane's Children*.

Modern Uzbekistan is a secular Muslim state with an authoritarian government. Tamerlane – the fourteenth-century warrior known in Uzbek as Amir Timur – has been declared the nation's father figure. With some poetic license, I have called the people of Uzbekistan "Tamerlane's children." This book is about some of them, the lives they lead, and the problems and challenges they face.

This book is not intended to be a comprehensive treatment of post-Soviet Uzbekistan. Instead, it presents a look at what I found to be the most interesting personalities, issues, and events I came across during the time I lived there.

The book is divided into two parts.

Part One consists of seven chapters, each one fairly able to stand apart from the other. These dispatches are the journalistic fruit of the reporting I did in Uzbekistan. Earlier incarnations of some of these dispatches appeared on National Public Radio and Public Radio International and in the *New Yorker* magazine. Part One begins with 9/11 and ends with a piece about cotton, Uzbekistan's critical agricultural commodity. In between are profiles of two of the most engaging people I met in Uzbekistan – a pop star and a horse trainer – as well as pieces about Islam (Uzbekistan is home to the oldest Qur'an in the world) and about love, Uzbek-style (based on hundreds of interviews on that topic conducted by the staff of Tashkent's Ilkhom Theatre).

Part Two begins with a free-wheeling dispatch, an essay, of sorts, about life in contemporary Uzbekistan. I attempt to give the reader a sense of what it is like to live there, through my own experiences and through the experience of others. It is part narration, part transcription, part illustration, and all, hopefully, elucidation. Part Two is based on a personal diary I kept, on my reporter's notebooks, and on transcripts of some of the interviews I conducted in Uzbekistan. At times, Part Two is, and is intended to be, subjective. I do not attempt to conceal my opinion. As an American, I found living in Uzbekistan to be fascinating, difficult, maddening, frustrating, occasionally uplifting, and often sad. Part Two will explain why – in my words and in the words of people I met and interviewed. Part Two ends with an update of key developments in Uzbekistan through 2005, and a prognosis for the future.

It is difficult to acknowledge everyone who contributed to this book. There are dozens of Uzbek friends, acquaintances, and colleagues who assisted me, but many of them would not want to be acknowledged in print. They know who they are, and I thank them for helping me to understand Uzbekistan. Among the expats I encountered in Tashkent, special thanks go to Josh Machleder of Internews, who knows far more about Uzbekistan than I ever will; Kevin Griffith and Paula Volk, Peace Corps volunteers who took me to the provinces and showed me a side of Uzbek life I otherwise would never have seen; and Penny Krumm, my friend and running partner, who helped keep me sane. Thanks, too, to William Fierman of Indiana University, who provided long-distance counsel on either end of my Uzbek adventure. And to Robert Mandel and Steve Salemson, without whose support this book would not have seen the light of day. And a heartfelt million thanks to Sally Davies: for trekking to Uzbekistan, and for holding down the fort on the home front while we were in Tashkent.

My wife, Eriko Hibi, contributed more than anybody else to this book. Without her, I never would have gone to Uzbekistan in the first place. Without her, while there I would have been deprived of a sounding-board that was both insightful and wise. Without her, Uzbekistan would have been only half the experience that it was.

My son, Ariel, essentially grew up in Tashkent. He came there when he was two and left when he was five. His first childhood memories will be of Uzbekistan. I hope, when he is older, this book will keep those memories fresh. His sister, Katrina, was conceived in Tashkent and, as a baby-turning-into-toddler, helped to lighten the psychic load of living there. It is to her this book is dedicated.

Part One

Part One

1

9/11

The Yunusabad tennis complex is not, strictly speaking, the seat of power in Uzbekistan, but the place does have a certain panache. It rests on a large swath of land near the center of Tashkent, the capital, right next to the television tower, a rocket-like spire of Soviet design that at 1,230 feet dominates the city's skyline, much as the Twin Towers once overlooked Manhattan. Yunusabad, completed in 1994, is a world-class facility, spiffier than Flushing Meadows. It boasts outdoor and indoor arenas, plexiplave courts, and, in the spirit of good public health, a building filled with stomatological services. One can book a teeth cleaning along with court time.

Yunusabad faces Amir Timur street, a boulevard named after Tamerlane, the fourteenth-century Samarkand warrior who, in post-Soviet Uzbekistan, has supplanted Lenin and Marx as the father figure of the country. In the anxious days following 9/11, when war was in the air – Uzbekistan borders Afghanistan – Yunusabad-on-Tamerlane was on alert, and the tennis club, notwithstanding its nongovernmental mantle, oddly, had a role to play.

Yunusabad, at the time, was home to the President's Cup, an annual event on the ATP – the men's professional tennis tour. Despite the poverty and remoteness of Uzbekistan, the competition drew top male competitors from across the world.

The man who built Yunusabad, and the man behind the cup, is Islam Abduganievich Karimov, tennis amateur, former Soviet Communist Party boss, and the first and only president of the independent Republic of Uzbekistan.

Karimov is serious about his tennis. Much as golf defined Eisenhower or horseback riding Reagan, tennis is central to Karimov's persona. A glossy coffee-table book of Karimov photographs, sanctioned by Karimov himself and published in 1998 on the occasion of his sixtieth birthday,[1] has a two-page spread of the President at play: a solid, silver-haired man with a flash of gold in his smile, dressed in white shirt and shorts, brandishing a Wilson racket.

Henry Dashevsky, his former coach, said Karimov has been known to practice four times a week. "His forehand is beautiful," Dashevsky said. "His backhand is good, maybe better than his forehand. His serve is good, and his smash is very good."

According to Dashevsky, Karimov volleys with visiting foreign dignitaries, drubbing, for instance, the presidents of Kazakhstan and Latvia.

Dashevsky said it is not just that Karimov loves tennis. He sees the game as an important political weapon – a weapon to inhibit the spread of Islamic fundamentalism in Uzbekistan, a secular but largely Muslim state that, since independence in 1991, has faced an on-again, off-again Islamic insurgency.

"During the last years many mosques were constructed in Uzbekistan," said Dashevsky, "and children were taken there and they studied religion and it was Karimov's decision that there should be some alternative to this, that children should have some other place to go."

And that place was the tennis court. Since the mid-1990s, Karimov has built more than four hundred tennis courts across Uzbekistan, a public works project with national security implications. Marat Kurmatov, director of the Tashkent division of the Uzbek Fund for the Support of Tennis Development, said the country spends "tens of thousands of dollars annually" on tennis infrastructure, a large sum for a nation that, according to the United Nations Development Programme, ranks as the poorest in per capita GDP among the countries of Central and Eastern Europe and the former Soviet Union.[2]

Interestingly, Rustam Inoyatov, Chairman of Uzbekistan's KGB – now renamed the SNB, or National Security Service – is president of the Uzbekistan Tennis Federation.

Among Uzbekistan's new tennis facilities is a club in a small provincial hub called Gulistan, about a ninety-minute drive from Tashkent. I asked the town's deputy mayor, Kamolitdin Okbutaev, to talk about the connection between tennis and internal security in Uzbekistan. He told me that if kids spend their free time playing tennis "they won't get involved in smoking or drugs or prostitution or with religious extremism and terrorism." "Sportsmen," he declared, "love their country."

"Better tennis rackets than military rockets," Karimov has said.

The terrorist strikes against New York and Washington took place on Day Two of the 2001 President's Cup tournament. As the world's major media covered the events in America live, state-controlled Uzbek TV stayed fixed on Yunusabad's center court; not until the following day were images of the World Trade Center and the Pentagon shown. In the meantime, Karimov prepared his response. On the Sunday after September 11, at the President Cup's closing ceremonies, Karimov ordered a minute of silence for America's victims, transforming Yunusabad into the venue for the Uzbek government's most significant public expression of sympathy toward the United States.

There was no doubt that Uzbekistan would condemn the terrorist actions and not much surprise that Karimov went on to lend the Americans an airbase, Karshi-Khanabad, for use in the approaching military campaign in Afghanistan. In February 1999, Tashkent was hit by a series of car bombs, which were thought to be targeted at Karimov. At least sixteen people died and scores were injured. Karimov escaped harm because, it is said, he was delayed in arriving at the Cabinet of Ministers building, one of the places attacked.

The February bombings were Uzbekistan's equivalent of the World Trade Center attacks, albeit much smaller in scale. People were outraged and scared. In a country where Muslims make up nearly ninety per cent of the population, Islamic extremists were blamed, accused of trying to turn Karimov's secular state into another Iran or Taliban-style Afghanistan. Terrorists, Karimov said, "should be shot in the head, and if necessary, I'll shoot them myself."[3]

The President initiated a security crackdown that continues to this day. Human-rights activists estimate that forty thousand policemen patrol the streets of Tashkent now; ten years ago, that number policed the entire country. Roadblocks and document checks are common. In the fight against fundamentalism, mosques have been stripped of loudspeakers to mute the public broadcast of the call to prayer, and thousands of Muslims have been jailed for professing their religion in a manner unsanctioned by the state. These measures augmented the pre-existing authoritarian order, in which a free press and political opposition were stifled. (The law prohibits publicly insulting the President in Uzbekistan.[4]) As for democracy, in the last presidential election, in 2000, Karimov's nominal rival announced that he had voted for Karimov.

Yet, in the period following the Tashkent bombings through 9/11 and its immediate aftermath, Karimov remained, at least on the streets of Tashkent, a benevolent despot – some called him "Papa" – who secured the social order. "If Islam Abduganievich were removed from power, there would be a fundamentalist government here within six months," one doctor told me. "I would happily show my documents ten times a day if that would guarantee peace and stability here," a businessman declared.

"I support Karimov and his policies," said a woman university professor, herself a Muslim. "I feel safe and secure here. I can go out at all hours and walk the streets. That wasn't the case several years ago. It is true that the police control things, but we do have personal freedom here. We can do what we want. As for human rights, I'm sure there are problems, but I don't see it. And neither do most people here."

The February 1999 bombings ruffled more than the internal political terrain of Uzbekistan. They triggered a significant upturn in military cooperation between Tashkent and Washington and laid the groundwork for the military alliance that would appear, with thunderbolt swiftness and resonance, in the weeks following 9/11.

The collapse of the Soviet Union in 1991 had dealt American diplomacy new strategic opportunities, and Central Asia was one of them. The region is bloating with reserves of oil and gas; it is the welcome mat to South Asia – to Afghanistan, Pakistan, and India; and it is situated at the underbelly of Russia, on the historic Silk Road, next door to China: prime post-Cold-War real estate for the purveyors of US foreign policy. In Soviet times, the US had not been welcomed to the neighborhood. With the so-called "Stans" – Kazakhstan, Kyrgyzstan, Tajikistan, Turkmenistan, and Uzbekistan (the most populous) – set loose, Washington was free, and often encouraged, to come visit. It was the beginning of a new "Great Game," the moniker used to describe the intense rivalry between tsarist Russia and Victorian Britain for control of the area in the eighteenth and nineteenth centuries.[5]

Secretary of State James Baker was the first high-ranking American official to visit the region, in February 1992. Uzbekistan, he said afterwards, was among a handful of countries that for many Americans "were just obscure names on a map just a year ago; now they stand in the front ranks of our efforts to enlarge the world's community of stable, democratic nations."

"This was my first-ever visit to several of these states," Baker told a congressional committee after his visit. "I return convinced that we face a once-in-a-century opportunity to shape the course of history and to define a new age for our children and grand-children. And, I am convinced that it is an opportunity that we, in concert with our allies, must seize."[6]

The website of the US Embassy in Tashkent – <www.usem-bassy.uz> – was one of the few sources that regularly chronicled the burgeoning American–Uzbek relationship. Things, at first, developed slowly, the website said. Washington's focus was elsewhere – in Iraq, in the Balkans, on the Israeli–Palestinian dispute. After Baker's visit, not much happened until 1996, when William Perry, the US Secretary of Defense, came calling on Karimov. That same year, the website said, Karimov visited Washington "on a private visit" and met with Perry, Energy Secretary Hazel O'Leary, and President Bill Clinton.

In 1997, Uzbek and American armed forces participated in exercises sponsored by NATO's "Partnership for Peace" program.

A year later, in October 1998, Anthony Zinni became the first US Central Command Commander-in-Chief to visit Uzbekistan. Two months earlier, Taliban forces had seized a chunk of territory on the Afghan side of the Amu Darya river, which separates Uzbekistan from Afghanistan. "Taliban Jars Central Asia," one newspaper headline read.[7] In response the US sent Zinni, who oversaw new joint military exercises. He came with the Tenth Mountain Division,[8] which after 9/11 would stake out a beachhead at Karshi-Khanabad.

Zinni returned to Uzbekistan twice in 1999, according to the US Embassy website: in May, three months after the Tashkent bombings, and again in December, after a summer offensive by the Islamic Movement for Uzbekistan (IMU), the organization blamed for the Tashkent attacks. That same year American Special Forces – Green Berets – for the first time set up shop at former Soviet facilities to help train Uzbekistan's army in its fight against Islamic extremists.[9] The IMU, which was intent on overturning Uzbekistan's existing political order, had scared Karimov. Tashkent needed American military know-how, and America was more than ready to respond.

The pace of cooperation quickened. In April 2000, Secretary of State Madeleine Albright traveled to Uzbekistan. This was especially welcome news for Karimov, who had visited Washington just the year before, only to be slighted by President Clinton, who failed to meet privately with the Uzbek leader during a summit marking NATO's fiftieth anniversary. The snub was wrapped in velvet, for Clinton sat next to Karimov at one of the NATO meetings,[10] and the Uzbek President did meet with other top US government officials. However, the absence of a one-on-one Oval Office session was intended to signal Washington's discomfort with Uzbekistan's human rights record,[11] and foreshadowed a dance that would only become more difficult with time as the US sought to square two competing interests: the necessity to secure Uzbekistan's cooperation in the war against terrorism, and the moral desire to press Karimov to clean up his human rights portfolio.

The Tashkent embassy website listed a spate of bilateral developments in 2000: the US delivered military transport vehicles to Uzbekistan worth US$2.65 million; Secretary Albright announced that the US would provide approximately US$3 million in assistance for equipment and training to help Uzbekistan combat terrorism and illicit trafficking in weapons of mass destruction, conventional arms, and narcotics; the State Department formally designated the IMU as a foreign terrorist organization; and in September 2000 – one year before 9/11 – there came The Man – General Tommy Franks – Zinni's successor, the down-to-earth, broad-shouldered warrior who would command military operations against the Taliban and al Qaeda in Afghanistan and later in Iraq.

Franks returned to Uzbekistan in May 2001 for meetings with Karimov and senior Uzbek military leaders. His comments, delivered shortly after arriving in Tashkent, indicated just how far US–Uzbek relations had come in the ten years since the Soviet collapse. The infrastructure for post-9/11 cooperation was in place.

"Let me say at this point that the relationship between the military of the United States of America and that of Uzbekistan remains excellent," Franks observed. "That relationship has grown over the years and I would anticipate that it will continue to grow even stronger in the future."[12]

"On several occasions already this year, we have had American Special Forces here, conducting joint training exercises with the Uzbek forces," Franks continued. "And within the next month or two we will have another exercise involving the joint training of American and Uzbek special operating forces ... And yes, intelligence information is shared on a continual basis."

Then came 9/11. John Herbst was the US Ambassador in Tashkent.

"I was in the Embassy when the first plane hit the World Trade Center," Herbst told me.[13] "My wife Nadya called me a few minutes after it happened with the news. Still watching television when the second plane hit, she called me immediately. Like many others, I understood at that instant that we were under terrorist assault. I immediately asked my Deputy Chief of Mission, Molly O'Neal, to assemble all members of the Embassy Emergency Action Committee [EAC], whose function is to prepare the mission for all crises and to oversee security. As some members had left for the evening, the EAC did not meet until an hour and a half later, when we ordered additional security precautions."

Concrete barricades quickly appeared on the street bordering the embassy. The sidewalk fronting the complex was closed off, as was an adjacent lane of street traffic. More armed guards patrolled the area. And shortly thereafter workmen began constructing a wall around the embassy, as well as a bomb-proof reception booth to process incoming visitors.

Until 9/11, the facility had been surrounded by a fence.

Herbst said he had two main responsibilities after the terrorist attacks: "The first was to maintain the security of the embassy and all Americans in Uzbekistan. The other was to develop relations with the Government of Uzbekistan [GOU] in a way that would facilitate our war on terrorism. The first step in maintaining security was frequent meetings of the Emergency Action Committee. In the weeks after 9/11 we met daily and, as required by events, more often. The purpose of the meetings was to monitor events and to react to them with appropriate security measures. During the weeks after 9/11 and the start of military operations in Afghanistan, there were many rumors and reports about possible terrorist actions against Americans in Uzbekistan. We also followed closely the security precautions taken by the GOU and the attitudes of Uzbek citizens to our operations in Afghanistan and towards us. We received excellent security cooperation from the GOU. We also found that the Uzbek people remained friendly toward us throughout this period. We maintained close touch with Americans around the country both to be sure that we knew what they were hearing and to inform them of the latest public information."

Herbst said the embassy considered the question of whether to order the evacuation of diplomatic personnel and dependents. He decided the security situation did not warrant that step. "In fact, most of the embassy community felt basically secure throughout this period," Herbst said. "The unease some felt was usually due to phone calls from family and friends back home, who had recently discovered that Uzbekistan bordered Afghanistan."

That unease did have one consequence: in late September, American Peace Corps volunteers serving in Uzbekistan – about 150 of them – were pulled out of the country. Mark Asquino, who then served as the embassy spokesman, said Washington, not Ambassador Herbst, made the decision to evacuate. Herbst believed the move was unfounded. "Parents were concerned about their kids," Asquino said, "and the parents contacted their congressmen, who contacted the Peace Corps director." Asquino said the evacuation order "had little to do with the situation on the ground ... But we didn't fight it." According to Asquino, the Peace Corps pullout rattled the nerves of local Uzbeks, who believed that if the Americans were leaving, something really bad was in the offing.

What was imminent was war in Afghanistan. Herbst said his embassy was directly involved in the critical job of securing Uzbekistan's assistance for American operations against the Taliban and al Qaeda.

"It became clear soon after 9/11 that al Qaeda was responsible for the attacks, and al Qaeda was based in Afghanistan," Herbst said. "Three days after the attacks, we sent a message to Washington outlining how we thought Uzbekistan might be helpful to any military operations in Afghanistan. We learned immediately that military planners were thinking along the same lines. We later learned that as part of the planning for military operations in Afghanistan, Washington wanted to be sure that our forces had a search and air rescue [SAR] capability for the entire country – to locate and extract American troops in danger. To provide this coverage in northern Afghanistan, a base in Uzbekistan would be ideal. Use of Uzbek airspace for carrying supplies for operations in Afghanistan was also important. Five days after we sent in our cable, President Bush called President Karimov to discuss cooperation in the war on terrorism. A week later, Under Secretary of State John Bolton arrived to discuss the same subject."

Initially, Herbst said, Karimov appeared reluctant to agree to an American request to set up a base. "There seemed to be two concerns. The first was that we would not complete the job in Afghanistan: we would initiate unsuccessful action that would leave the Taliban in power, and angry at Tashkent for providing support for our operations."

"The Uzbeks were also concerned about the possible reaction from Moscow to a decision to permit the American military to set up shop in Uzbekistan," Herbst said. "Russian President Putin's statement in late September, expressing understanding for a temporary American military presence in Central Asia to conduct operations in Afghanistan, partly allayed these concerns."

"By the time of Under Secretary Bolton's departure from Tashkent," Herbst said, "the GOU had agreed not only to military overflights, but also to our setting up a base at Karshi-Khanabad for SAR flights."

K-2, as Karshi-Khanabad was called, is situated some ninety miles north of the Uzbek–Afghan border on an isolated, arid piece of land that was once home to a Soviet airbase. From K-2, military aircraft can reach any point inside Afghanistan within two hours.

Herbst said one incentive Bolton offered Karimov during their talks was a US$80 million increase in economic and military assistance. "But the main reason for the GOU decision to allow us to set up a base was the prospect of closer ties with the US, something that it had been seeking for years. Fiercely jealous of their independence, the Uzbeks saw a closer relationship with the distant US as a way to strengthen their position in the region. Moreover, the

Uzbeks understood that a successful American campaign in Afghanistan would deal a real blow to their own homegrown extremist group, the Islamic Movement of Uzbekistan, which had been conducting terrorist acts in Uzbekistan since 1999. The IMU was based in Afghanistan and was actively involved with al Qaeda in fighting the Northern Alliance prior to 9/11."

The Northern Alliance was a coalition of ethnic groups in northern Afghanistan that had united for the purpose of fighting the Taliban. Included in the alliance was a large contingent of ethnic Uzbeks.

Secretary of Defense Donald Rumsfeld arrived in Tashkent a week after Under Secretary Bolton. Rumsfeld met with Karimov on 5 October. "By the time of his arrival," Herbst said, "we had already begun to set up our base at Karshi-Khanabad. With Secretary Rumsfeld's visit, we publicly announced our intention to run search and air missions from K-2. As a result of the visit, it was also agreed that Special Operations Forces could also be inserted into Afghanistan from K-2. These forces provided vital liaison with the Northern Alliance."

On 7 October, on the heels of Rumsfeld's departure from Uzbekistan, the US commenced military action in Afghanistan. Among Uzbeks the anxiety was palpable, as people tried to adjust to the geopolitical earthquake 9/11 had wrought. Al Qaeda may have struck the distant American homeland, but the repercussions for Uzbekistan were immediate and clear. You could hear them even in Tashkent, where the rumble of American military aircraft filled the skies, shaking the nerves of the people below.

The worry on the street was whether the war would spread northward to Uzbekistan: whether the Taliban would cross the border and, as it had publicly threatened, rain down a jihad on

Uzbek soil, payback for helping the Americans; and whether the IMU, which, as Herbst said, had links to Osama bin Laden's al Qaeda network, would let loose its cells inside Uzbekistan. Nobody knew just how strong the IMU was or how much sympathy the group had garnered among Uzbekistan's Muslim population. But Karimov recognized the fresh threat of the IMU and the general apprehension about instability and even potential war. The Uzbek President may have supported the US-led war against terrorism, but he did so gingerly, trying, in public pronouncements, to calm his nation, to lower the collective blood pressure, to create the impression, not wholly true, that Uzbekistan's aid to America was altruistic and less than vigorous.

The day after American and British forces went into action, Karimov put his foreign-policy advisers on TV. Their objective: to reassure the nation. There was no truth to reports that Taliban troops were massing at the Uzbek border, the advisers said. The war in Afghanistan, they said, is a war against terror, not against Islam or the Afghan people. It is a campaign, they maintained, that many Islamic and Arab leaders supported, including Libya's Colonel Muammar Qaddafi. Abdulaziz Komilov, the Uzbek Foreign Minister, noted that Qaddafi "said the US is fully in its right to attack."[14] It was an innovative spin on the American cause.

In his public comments, Karimov said again and again that American aircraft based at Khanabad could only be used for humanitarian purposes and search-and-rescue missions. Commando units, he said, could not be stationed in Uzbekistan, and offensive operations could not be conducted from Uzbek territory.[15] He was speaking with a wink and a nod. The latter assertion, regarding Special Forces, ran contrary to the agreement quietly reached with Rumsfeld. And Karimov also was reported to have privately told the Americans he was open to an even larger US presence in Uzbekistan "if a generous package of assistance and security guarantees was provided by Washington."[16]

On 12 October, the US and Uzbekistan issued a joint statement announcing that Tashkent would allow American forces to use Uzbek territory for humanitarian purposes "in the first instance."[17] The door was now publicly, albeit discreetly, open to second-instance, non-humanitarian missions, presumably of an offensive nature. In return, Karimov received reassurances that if Uzbekistan got into real trouble the US would probably send in the Marines. The statement stressed that the two countries had established a "qualitatively new relationship." "We recognize the need to work closely together in the campaign against terrorism," the statement said. "This includes the need to consult on an urgent basis about appropriate steps to address the situation in the event of a direct threat to the security or territorial integrity of the Republic of Uzbekistan."[18]

Karimov's decision to side with the United States after 9/11 seemed to have had the endorsement of his people. In October 2001, in the days after US forces began to attack Afghanistan, I spoke with dozens of Tashkent residents, on the streets, in cabs, in the bazaars. There were a few discordant voices, all of them Muslim. "The hell with it," said one Muslim street vendor. "Who needs war?" Another man, a trader, said, "We need to defend our brother Muslims."

But mostly there was support, for a combination of reasons. The lure of American culture and prosperity had permeated the country. Coca-Cola, skateboards, Britney Spears posters, tee shirts made in the USA – these had become staples of Uzbek life, especially in the capital. I once saw, in a Tashkent park, a Muslim man kneeling down on an American flag beach towel at prayer time. The Americans also had the advantage of having opposed seventy-plus years of Soviet communism. In the new Great Game, where the US had supplanted Britain as a rival to Russia, the red, white, and blue was a welcome antidote to the legacy of Kremlin domination.

And then there was Afghanistan. A million-and-a-half Uzbeks live there, mainly in the north. Rashid Dostam, a leader of the Northern Alliance, is an ethnic Uzbek and a Karimov partisan. Uzbeks also resent the influx of heroin and opium from Afghanistan, which is swallowing up increasing numbers of Uzbek youths. Compounding these sentiments is the memory of a bygone war, the one unleashed by the Kremlin. Tashkent was the base of operations for that other Afghan conflict which Leonid Brezhnev began in 1979 and Mikhail Gorbachev ended ten years later.

That war was Uzbekistan's Vietnam. Moscow filled the ranks of the Red Army with Central Asian conscripts. Talat Muradov, a former Soviet intelligence officer and president of Uzbekistan's largest veterans group, told me sixty-five thousand citizens of the USSR living in Uzbekistan were forced to serve in Afghanistan. More than fifteen hundred died, he said. For the survivors and their families, the memory of fighting the Afghans is clear as a snapshot, and the feelings are hard.

"Those people are animals, nothing less," one veteran, a former helicopter pilot, told me. "All of Central Asia will benefit from eliminating the Taliban ... They need to be destroyed."

By March 2002, the Taliban had been defeated, or at least disbursed. A new interim government had been set up in Kabul, the Afghan capital, led by Hamid Karzai, an ethnic Pashtun who led one of the largest tribes in the southern part of the country.

As for Karimov, he was en route to Washington for a meeting with President George W. Bush. Bush told Karimov that security cooperation between Tashkent and Washington had "opened a new chapter in US–Uzbekistan relations."[19] To underline the point, the two sides signed an unprecedented "Strategic Partnership" agreement. The US promised "to regard with grave concern any external threat" to Uzbekistan and also announced a tripling of foreign aid to US$160 million. The US Export-Import Bank granted Uzbekistan US$55 million in new credits. Secretary of State Colin Powell, who lunched with Karimov, signed an agreement to purchase land in Tashkent for the construction of a new, larger, and more secure US embassy. Karimov, Powell said, was "a solid coalition partner."[20]

As for that nettlesome issue of human rights, the dance continued. President Bush, in his meeting with Karimov, "stressed the importance of progress in human rights to the future growth and strength of Uzbekistan and to US–Uzbekistan relations."[21] Uzbekistan, in the Strategic Partnership agreement, agreed to "intensify the democratic transformation of its society politically and economically."[22]

"There are problems with respect to human rights in Uzbekistan," Powell told a congressional committee, "and we will not shrink from discussing them."[23]

John Herbst, the US Ambassador to Uzbekistan, said his "most difficult and frustrating challenge was working to persuade the Government of Uzbekistan to undertake serious political and economic reform." Hardest of all, he said, was human rights, "where the country's record was very poor."

"During President Karimov's visit to Washington, our two governments signed a Memorandum of Understanding committing the GOU to making progress on reform. Congress later passed legislation requiring us to certify progress in order for Uzbekistan to continue receiving assistance from us. In the first half of 2002, the GOU made clear, if not large, progress on both political and economic reform."

Herbst said the number of political prisoners had dropped by a few hundred (human-rights groups estimated the total number to be between six and seven thousand); an Uzbek human-rights organization was officially registered, albeit on the eve of Karimov's White House meeting;[24] and Uzbekistan, Herbst said, had fulfilled many parts of an agreement with the International Monetary Fund concerning economic reform.

"But by the summer of 2002," Herbst said, "the positive trend largely stopped." "The overall record was troublesome, and worse. We were particularly upset by the continuing deaths (of Uzbek prisoners) in detention. On the economic side, after a promising start in 2002, things began to turn sour in July with the introduction of restrictions on trade."

"We made it clear," Herbst said, "by constant, vigorous diplomacy and some public statements – throughout the remainder of my time in Tashkent [until July, 2003] and since – that this would prevent improvements in the bilateral relationship and could affect our assistance."

In February 2004, the US Department of State issued its annual report on human rights in Uzbekistan.[25] Among the conclusions: "Uzbekistan is an authoritarian state with limited civil rights. The Constitution provides for a presidential system with separation of powers among the executive, legislative, and judicial branches; however, in practice, President Islam Karimov and the centralized executive branch that serves him dominate political life and exercise nearly complete control over the other branches. Following a January 2002 referendum judged to be neither free nor fair, the President's term in office was extended by 2 years. Previous elections were neither free nor fair ...

"The Government's human rights (record) remained very poor, and (the Government) continued to commit numerous serious abuses ...

"The Government employed official and unofficial means to restrict severely freedom of speech and the press, and an atmosphere of repression stifled public criticism of the Government ...

"Although the law prohibits such practices, both the police and the NSS routinely tortured, beat and otherwise mistreated detainees to obtain confessions or incriminating information ...

"Authorities continued to arrest and detain human rights activists arbitrarily ... "

In July 2004, the State Department announced that the US had decided to reduce assistance to the government of Uzbekistan because of the lack of progress in human-rights, political, and economic reform. Human-rights activists, both inside and outside Uzbekistan,welcomed the decision. It "has been long in coming," said one.[26] The US, they argued, had not pressed Karimov's regime on issues of reform vigorously enough in the years since 9/11. In their view, it was Karimov, and not George W. Bush – or John Herbst – who had led the dance on human rights. Had the US done a better job, there might have been more progress. Nonetheless, the cutback in aid was a step, they said, in the right direction, a new move that eventually might encourage Uzbekistan to reverse course in order to recapture the full affection of its American partner.

As things turned out, however, continued disagreements over human rights would chill relations between Tashkent and

Washington even further and lead, in August 2005, to Uzbekistan's ordering the US out of the Karshi-Khanabad airbase. The catalyst was Andijon, in Uzbekistan's Ferghana Valley, where the Uzbek authorities in May of that year forcefully put down a public gathering, killing hundreds, and sending hundreds more into refugee camps in nearby Kyrgyzstan. The events in Andijon jarred Karimov's regime and altered the nature of US–Uzbek relations. More on all that in the final two chapters of this book.

2

Amir Timur

In the center of Tashkent there is a park. It is a lovely place – for parks are rare in Tashkent. When the weather is nice, people gather in this park, as they have gathered there for decades. They do so mostly because of the trees: the park is filled with them, with lush, green foliage – also uncommon in Tashkent – that provides ample shade against the blistering Central Asian sun.

At the center of this park – which Uzbeks call "the Square" – is a magnificent monument: an equestrian statue that sits atop a massive pedestal. A muscular steed, with one hoof proudly raised, dominates the space. Mounting the horse is the figure of Tamerlane – Amir Timur – the ancient warrior and national hero of post-Soviet Uzbekistan. Timur's right hand is outstretched, as if acknowledging the masses. His face is stern, serious, contemplative. His cape flails back with the wind. A long sabre hangs at his side.

The monument was dedicated in 1992, on the second anniversary of Uzbekistan's independence. Islam Abduganievich Karimov, the new president, spoke: "Amir Timur the Great has returned to his motherland as a result of obtaining its independence and sovereignty."

During Soviet times, Timur was off limits, mostly derided as a feudal villain, a cruel, anti-socialist predator who had killed tens of thousands of the proletarian and peasant masses.

"Our people, who for many years were in the clutches of colonialists, were deprived of the possibility to revere their great compatriot and to pay due respect to his historical merits," Karimov said.

The Amir Timur Square monument was the first of many such shrines to materialize throughout Uzbekistan after independence. A statue appeared in Samarkand – the seat of Timur's regime – on 18 October 1996: "Comprehending Amir Timur is understanding oneself," Karimov said. And in Shakhrisabz, Timur's birthplace, on the same day: "If anybody would like to know who the Uzbek is," Karimov said, "wherein lies the power and might of the Uzbek nation, wherein lies its justice and boundless potential, what contribution was made to world development and through it all to realize its faith in the future, then they must remember the personality of Amir Timur."[27]

The year 1996 – the 660th anniversary of Timur's birth – also saw the opening, in Tashkent, of a museum dedicated solely to the memory and achievements of Tamerlane.

All this let loose a cult of Timur, memorializing a historical figure known for his empire building, administrative skills, intelligence, architectural grandeur, and brutality. No longer were Lenin and Marx the nation's state icons, as they had been when the

Fig.1. Historian Edvard Rtveladze.

USSR was around. Now Tamerlane was the father figure of Uzbekistan.

The square in the middle of Tashkent had seen its share of heroes come and go. Tamerlane was merely the latest. All told, eleven monuments had occupied the park's central stage. The first was Konstantin Kaufman, the Russian general who had conquered much of Central Asia in the second half of the nineteenth century and who had ruled the area for nearly two decades. Later, in 1924, came the Hammer and Sickle, symbols of Soviet power. Then came Joseph Stalin. Eventually Karl Marx. Finally, Amir Timur.

History is fleeting. Tashkenters had seen the idols come and go. When, in 1991, communism fell into disgrace, Karl Marx was history. So was Lenin, whose statue, situated elsewhere in the city, was torn down. "We had an ideological gap which had to be filled in," said Edvard Rtveladze, a prominent historian. "Best of all, some outstanding figure, someone well known. Besides Amir Timur, no one suited this role."

"Now there is total eulogy of Amir Timur," Rtveladze said. "His activities must be studied well. In detail. I heard with my own ears some guy on TV say, and it was crazy, that when the Germans approached Moscow during World War II, Stalin ordered the remains of Amir Timur brought to Moscow, put them into a plane to circle the German troops, and only after that the Soviet army defeated the Germans. That is the level of the majority of literature published about Timur today. This is terrible. Awful."

Rtveladze was speaking in 1996 – the year of Timur – in a documentary film entitled *The End of an Era. Tashkent*, produced by Mark Weil, director of the Ilkhom Theatre in Tashkent. I visited Rtveladze eight years later, in his office at the Fine Arts Scientific Research Institute of the Academy of Arts of Uzbekistan.

Rtveladze is Uzbekistan's foremost Tamerlane scholar. I wondered whether the decision to make Amir Timur the nation's father figure was a controversial one, given Timur's record as a brutal warrior. Historians estimate hundreds of thousands of people died at the hands of Timur's army. According to Beatrice Forbes Manz, a leading Western expert on Tamerlane, the conqueror's forces carried out "the massacres of city populations designed to rival those of Chinggis Khan."[28]

"Was there any protest of the decision to elevate Timur?" I asked.

Rtveladze, a wiry man with green eyes and a weathered face, leaned forward on his desk. It was Karimov's decision, he said, and his alone. "Literally this initiative to create the cult of Timur as a national hero came from him."

"By the way," he added, "our President knows history very well. I have often discussed history personally with him, on various excursions to our museums, and he has sufficient historical knowledge to determine who should be the national symbol of Uzbekistan."

"Was there any opposition to the choice of Timur, given his violent track record?" I asked.

"There was among scholars," Rtveldadze said. "Among the country's intelligentsia there were discussions that Timur shouldn't be made a national hero because he was a cruel conqueror of other peoples, and so forth. But, you know, history is complicated and multi-dimensional. It is difficult to evaluate the role of the individual in history."

Rtveladze took a drag on a cigarette, one of many he smoked during our conversation. His office overlooks the Cabinet of Ministers building, the functional arm of Karimov's government. And overlooking Rtveladze, on the wall above his desk, is a photograph of Edvard Rtveladze with the Uzbek President.

Rtveladze said Amir Timur had lived in difficult times. Few historical leaders and few historical epochs can offer up clean hands, he said. "For some reason there is an interesting tendency that whenever we talk about the personality of Timur, or Timur as a national hero, immediately attention is diverted to his negative side. But somehow, his positive features are ignored. But you know, dear Robert, that the well-being of America was built on the backs of ten million slaves, blacks, who were pirated away from Africa. Remember Oliver Cromwell in England, and the thousands of Brits who perished in his bourgeois revolution? Remember Robespierre? The Spanish Inquisition? Is all this any less cruel than Amir Timur?"

Rtveladze acknowledged he had misgivings over the elevation of Tamerlane to cult status in Uzbekistan, but not because of Tamerlane's ruthlessness. "I understood very well the epoch in which he lived. But I wondered how a historical figure who lived six centuries ago could become a unifying, strengthening factor in today's Uzbekistan. But I analyzed the history of Uzbekistan and analyzed its historical personalities. And you know what? There just wasn't any other figure who would work. Do you understand? There was nobody else."

In a speech in October 1996, Karimov explained his decision to lionize Timur, and addressed the issue of Timur's brutality.

"What does free and prosperous Uzbekistan need Amir Timur for?" Karimov asked. "Amir Timur created a powerful state ... Today, as we work towards strengthening the independence of Uzbekistan, Amir Timur is significant to us as the founder of this great state ... In the administration of his state Amir Timur used not only force. Unfortunately, some sources and research works emphasize just this point of view. Personally I am against it. If this state was formed and relied only on force it would not have lasted this long. It is fair to say that Amir Timur, in his ruling, relied on his mind and a solid legislative base."

Karimov went on to cite other reasons Uzbekistan needed Timur. Timur was a skillful diplomat who understood the need to cooperate with neighboring countries; Timur understood that international economic ties are important to nation building; Timur was a prodigious builder of mosques, markets, palaces, and other construction projects, which appeals to the current generation; Timur was a patron of science and education; and "Timur remembered one thing – a society cannot live without religion." He knew, Karimov said, "that people need faith. He said in his laws: 'I support Islam everywhere and always.'"[29]

Ironically, according to Tamerlane scholar Beatrice Forbes Manz, "Timur was not an Uzbek." The Uzbeks, she told me, started as a tribal confederation in the Aral Sea area, led by one of Chinggis Khan's relatives. Timur, she said, was from an entirely different tribe. He considered the Uzbek clan "less civilized" than his.

Manz has written a detailed history of Amir Timur called *The Rise and Rule of Tamerlane*.[30] In the book, Manz explains that, though Tamerlane conquered "most of the known world," his empire was "neither enormous nor secure" at the time of his death in 1405. In order to enhance their claim to power, Tamerlane's successors "actively cultivated the charisma of their ancestor as an integral part of their own legitimacy." There was no doubt, Manz argues, that Timur was a great and powerful leader, known near and far as a man with a wide scope of interests, a man of "extraordinary intelligence." His successors played this up and created "a legendary figure, equipped with an elaborate and partly supernatural genealogy."[31]

The myth of Timur, Manz says, "proved highly useful to the Turkic dynasties which followed the Timurids [Tamerlane's successors] in the Middle East and Central Asia, and it continued to flourish in the eastern Islamic world into the nineteenth century." And the myth of Timur has proved useful as well to Islam Karimov in contemporary Uzbekistan.

Of all the tribes and clans of Central Asia, it was only Amir Timur and his domain that achieved international fame. Certainly, Manz argues, the original tribe of Uzbeks did not attain such prestige and power. "The breadth of [Timur's] conquests and his reputation are major assets, both because they boost the prestige of Uzbekistan within Central Asia, and because they give it an independent place in world history." All this, Manz concludes, makes Timur "suitable for the role he now plays in Uzbekistan."[32]

One summer day, I visited Amir Timur Square to speak to Uzbeks about their national hero. It was hot and sunny. It is always hot and sunny in Tashkent in the summertime. Old men sat on benches playing chess. Families walked about. I approached a young man, nineteen years old, an ethnic Uzbek.

"Does Amir Timur have meaning for you?" I asked.

"Yes, of course," he replied. "Timur was the first to build Uzbekistan. He saved Europe from the Turks. We are proud of him."

Next, a twenty-eight-year-old Uzbek man who worked in the park as a groundskeeper.

"Is your life better now or in Soviet times?" I asked.

"It's better now," the man said. "You can go where you want."

"Does Timur have significance for you?"

"No. He's our, what's it called? He's our whatever."

I walked up to an old man who was wearing a baseball cap that said "Western Union" on it. He had just set up a chessboard on a park bench in front of the Timur statue.

"How old are you?"

"Oh, I'm still young. Sixty-three." He looked much older. His grizzled, wrinkled face was flecked with thin white stubble. His thin gray hair wildly flew out in various directions. The man, named Nikolai, said his father was Uzbek and his mother Chuvash (a Turkic ethnic group).

"Does Amir Timur have significance for you?"

"No," he said. "I have no use for him in my life. Fifty, seventy years went by, and look how we live right now. A million years have gone by without change. See, today people are poor and hungry, you understand. They put up a monument for this Timur, and he was just another tsar. He stole from the people and he murdered them."

"Is your life better now than it was in Soviet times?"

"It was better in Soviet times."

"Why?"

"Bread cost twenty kopecks. Sugar was seventy-eight kopecks. Now it costs five hundred rubles. It's as bad as it was under the Tsars. In Soviet times for six hundred rubles you could buy two tons of sugar. And now, what kind of a life do we have? It's not a life. It's torture. I come here to earn money to buy a piece of bread. I rent out a chessboard and I charge one hundred rubles." The man is confusing rubles, the money used in Uzbekistan under the Soviet Union, with the soum, the current Uzbek currency.

I then meet a seventy-three-year-old ethnic Uzbek, a former mining engineer. "Timur united us," he said. "He united all of Central Asia, to India and Afghanistan. He was very just. Very disciplined. He made the law equal for everyone. I've read a lot about him."

"Was your life better in Soviet times or now?" I asked.

A long pause.

"Well, it was better then. Because the law worked fairly then. There were problems, but things were better. The government defended the people more than it does now. The economy is worse now."

The man paused and looked down at the tape recorder in my hand.

"You're recording, yes? You shouldn't record. We don't do that. It's not allowed. It's dangerous."

With that the conversation ended.

A twenty-five-year-old Uzbek man was sitting on a bench in front of the Timur statue.

"Are things better for you now than they were before, under the Soviet Union?" I asked.

"It's a difficult question. What can I say? I guess things are better now."

"Why?"

"How can I explain it? We're free. During Soviet times you couldn't do want you want. Now we're free. You can go wherever you want without problems. In Soviet times, people who worked for the government were afraid even to go to their own mother's or father's funerals. And you couldn't go to mosques. If they saw you they'd demand your Communist Party card. But now, things are okay. Everything is open. You can do what you want. We go to the mosque freely. But earlier, under the USSR, you couldn't even say 'in the name of Allah.' Now you can."

I next approached a middle-aged woman, an ethnic Korean. "You know how things are," she said. "The economy has turned bad. For instance, I'm a doctor. I'm looking for work. Do you know how much they want to pay me? Eighteen thousand soum a month [about US$18]."

The woman laughs. "Transportation costs alone, the bus, the metro, would cost me twenty-four thousand. Can you imagine? And I'm not even talking about the cost of food, and other living expenses."

Nearby stood a photography booth, where two men and a woman were taking pictures of visitors in front of the Timur monument.

"Why do people want to have their picture taken here?" I asked.

One of the men replied, "This is the center of Tashkent. This is the only such monument here. So people want to show that they've visited the place."

"Are you all ethnic Russians?"

"Yes," the man said. "But he's a Tatar," nodding to his colleague.

"Does Amir Timur have significance for you?"

"No," said the man.

"None at all," said the woman.

"None," said the Tatar.

"Was your life better in Soviet times?"

"Of course," said the lady.

"Yes," said the Tatar.

"No," says the Russian, the youngest of the group.

"The youngest says no," I said.

They all laughed.

"He wasn't raised properly!" the woman joked.

The young Russian wavered: "The thing is, at the beginning it was okay when Uzbekistan became independent. Now they have beaten all the patriotism out of us. All of us Russians now want to leave, to emigrate to Russia."

I asked the woman why life was better under the Soviet Union.

"You could say we lived under communism then," she joked. "But the economy was better, our material life was much better than now. There was a social safety net. Now there isn't."

The Tatar added, "In school, in Soviet times, they used to teach us that Amir Timur was an evil conqueror like Hitler. And now he sits on a monument. They taught us in Soviet schools that he built everything out of blood. And now he's a national hero."

"How much does it cost to get your picture taken?" I asked.

"Seven hundred soum," the woman said. About seven dollars.

"Do you guys work here all day?"

"Yes, to 10 p.m."

"How's business?"

"From time to time its okay," she said.

"How much money do your earn each month?"

"About fifty thousand soum." Or fifty dollars.

"Can you live on that?" I asked.

"We have no other choice," the woman said. "We live."

I walked up to an elderly man in a tebeteika, the traditional Uzbek skullcap. He has a white moustache and is carrying a plastic bag with a chessboard inside.

"Excuse me, I'm a journalist from the United States."

"Oh, excellent! Come on. Let's talk!"

"Are you from Tashkent?"

"Yes. I studied here. Worked here. Now I'm retired on a pension and I come to this park to play chess."

"Do you happen to know," I asked, "before the Amir Timur statue was put up here, what other statues were here?"

"First there was Kaufman, the governor of Tashkent. Then Stalin-bobo. Our grandfather. The Karl Marx. Now, our Amir Timur-bobo."

Bobo is Uzbek for "grandfather".

"Who was the best?" I asked.

"Everyone was the best in his own time. That's the truth."

"Even Stalin?"

"I repeat. Everyone was the best in his own time. Isn't that the truth? No doubt about it. Anyway, only time and history will judge. Time is the main judge."

"Does Amir Timur have significance for you?"

"We consider him our grandfather. Once they used to criticize him. Now time has passed. We're on the path to democracy, and that has permitted his resurrection. By the way, what's your name?"

"Robert."

"My name is Nurtoi. That means 'light,' a big light."

"Are you an Uzbek?"

"Kipchak. Uzbeks aren't one nation. We're made up of different nationalities, small nationalities who gathered together. We're just like the United States of America! A melting pot. Yes. Yes. Yes! Kipchaks are the light of the Uzbeks."

"Kipchak?"

"Kipchak. A very historic name. Have you ever heard of Chinggis Khan? His mother was a Kipchak. An Uzbechka. But Robert, let me tell you, I've played chess here with Americans. I love Americans. I praise them. Americans are a very rich and peaceful people. When you ask an American to play chess, they immediately agree. Others, they just sit, and think, 'Am I in the mood?' Anyway, you've got the Democratic convention going on now, right?"

"Yes, it just started today. In Boston."

"Kerry, John Kerry, will he win?"

"You've heard of him?"

"Yes. Yes. Let me give you my opinion. From me, Nurtoi. George Bush, he's the most progressive man, the most heroic president. What he has done, nobody else could do. John Kerry, he's just one-tenth the man Bush is. Why? Afghanistan. The Taliban were there. They threatened everybody. They were like Hitler. George Bush-bobo got it right. He understood them. They planned to take over Tajikistan. They had a map. Tajikistan. Kyrgyzstan. Uzbekistan. Kazakhstan. And Russia."

"Even Russia?"

"Yes, they made those plans. To take over Russia."

"Can I ask you how old you are?"

"I'm sixty-four."

"Was your life better in Soviet times, or now?"

"Every time has its pluses and minuses. Now, the economic situation isn't good. Why do I come here to play chess? I earn about one dollar a day. Or maybe a half dollar. People pay me to play with them. It's not much money. But we have democracy now. Freedom is more valuable than money. You understand? I'll tell you a story. Foreign tourists come to this square. Americans too. Once, not long ago, I saw two foreigners. They looked like Americans. As is my custom, I started to ask if they wanted to play chess. All of a sudden I heard this screaming, screaming in my language, Uzbek. It was the foreigners' guide, yelling at me, telling me I can't talk to the foreigners. I told her, 'I've had enough of that kind of rude behavior in Soviet times. We're on the path of democracy and capitalism now. Those old times are gone. Just tell the foreigners what I asked. I don't need any more of your Soviet ways.'"

"But tell me more. Are things better now for you, or were they better in Soviet days?"

"Things are difficult now. But I think with time things will be better. Of course, we'll never be a second America. Nobody can be another America. I watch the movies. I know what America is. America is a unique state. There won't be a second one. Maybe something similar to it. I hope with time things will be better here."

"Thanks very much for talking to me."

"Let's play chess!" he said.

"Sorry. Don't know how," I said.

"Okay. It was nice meeting you. Give my greetings to America. Whether the Democrats or Republicans win, I just hope for peace. As for George Bush, I respect him from the bottom of my soul. Remember, nobody else would do what he did in Afghanistan. He's this kind of man," he said, giving me a thumbs up. "Robert, I wish you good health. Goodbye."

3

Sevara of Uzbekistan

On the evening of the first day of Ramadan in Tashkent, capital of the secular Islamic republic called Uzbekistan, the crowd inside Mama's Fun Pub was cutting loose. A beefy deejay, black baseball cap akimbo, pranced about the nightclub's sound stage. Slithery, sweaty female torsos provocatively clad in hot pants, skintight skirts, and black leather halters undulated on the dance floor, rolling their exposed navels to the pulsating rhythms of electronically enhanced pop music. Young men, their eyes popping out, tried to keep pace. Nearby, bartenders doled out Heineken on tap. Cigarette smoke clouded the room. Laser lights cut through the fog, creating an otherworldly scene: heaven or hell, depending on the depth and direction of your religious predilection.

This was the Tashkent arts pack: young men and women, mostly Uzbek nationals, with a sprinkling of ethnic Russians.

Radio personalities. Record producers. Composers. Journalists. Singers. And a dose of chic, eager teenage wannabees.

The Russians at Mama's were part of Tashkent's dwindling Slavic population. When Uzbekistan was a Soviet socialist republic, Russians were the dominant political force. After the USSR collapsed in 1991, Uzbekistan declared independence, and the Russians suddenly became subservient. They found themselves living a kind of internal exile: displaced persons, buffeted about as ethnic Uzbeks seized virtually all key posts in politics, industry, and the arts. Stung by the turnaround, Russians by the thousands returned to the motherland. Those who remained, and their children, made the best of it, and Mama's Fun Pub accommodated.

The Uzbeks at Mama's were Muslim, as is some ninety per cent of Uzbekistan's twenty-five million people. The party girls and boys who filled the club that night challenged post-9/11 Muslim stereotypes. No fundamentalists here. No long-bearded men or ladies in burqas. Instead, on the dance floor, a carousing dark-haired enchantress in a skintight sequined pantsuit, her face indeed veiled, not by creed but in the name of fashion.

I came to Mama's Fun Pub that evening with a young Uzbek woman named Sevara Nazarkhan. Sevara is a bona fide pop celebrity, one of Uzbekistan's most famous singers. "Superstar" is how one Tashkent newspaper labels her. Her face adorns calendars and posters. She plays the Presidential Palace, appears on TV, and fields calls on radio talk shows. Heads turn when she walks down the street. Autograph seekers assault her, and the young men among them want to know whether she has a boyfriend. She is the subject of gab magazine profiles: "Question: Who are your favorite actors? Answer: Brandon Lee and Kevin Kostner. Question: What

Fig. 2. Sevara Nazarkhan. Photo: Bakhrom Primkulov.

is your favorite perfume? Answer: There are many, but I especially like Naomi.'"

Sevara is a Muslim, and a believer. Allah is her prophet. But her brand of Islam is supple. It indulges a lifestyle and career that, though not exactly J.Lo., does resemble the familiar American image of success and stardom in the entertainment industry. She has fame, a Western recording contract, and by Uzbek standards – the average monthly wage is twenty-some dollars – a fair amount of money.

I had met Sevara a few weeks before, invited by her manager and partner, Bakhrom Primkulov, to a recording studio, where she was fine-tuning her latest album. The studio was in a modest, single-story home in a mahalla – a residential neighborhood – near the Yunusabad tennis complex.

Sevara was inside the control room working with an engineer when I arrived. They sat behind a modern mixing board with a twenty-one-inch computer screen propped in front of them. "We're using a software program called Q-Base," the engineer said. A digital rendering of nineteen tracks of music filled the color monitor. A rack of Yamaha and Tascam audio components stood nearby. Pretty impressive for Uzbekistan.

The engineer tapped at the keyboard, and music filled the room.

"I don't think we should use that part," Sevara said, grimacing. "It's bad."

The engineer grabbed at the mouse, manipulated the computerized audio mix, pressed the space bar, and the music, slightly altered, played again. "We need to slow down the speed a bit," Sevara said.

"She's not only a performer," Bakhrom explained. "She also produces her own albums."

Sevara is a petite, pretty woman with long brown hair and skin that is Central Asian ruddy. Her eyes, dark brown, are also slightly oriental, a bequest to Uzbekistan's genetic stock from the Silk Road, which once linked the region to China. They are thoughtful yet whimsical eyes, both pensive and sentimental. "I am a serious person," Sevara says, "but also a romantic, as are most of the Uzbek people."

Sevara is only twenty-five, and a few pimples still mar her complexion. Her upper teeth are filled with shiny dental braces.

Sevara tells the engineer she wants to return to the studio to retake some voice tracks. Bakhrom brings her an ashtray, and she spits something out of her mouth. The pop star of Uzbekistan wears braces and chews gum.

Sevara's lyrics come straight from a book of traditional Uzbek poetry. The topic is lost love, and the grief that it can cause:

> Kimlarnidir khasrat jengadi,
> mjen toparman irodalik
> kurgim kelar sizni negadir.

"Grief can overtake someone," she sings. "I will find the strength to overcome. But I still want to see you, for some reason."

Sevara's art is deeply rooted in the Uzbek traditions. On the Silk Road it was the men who moved the caravans, but it was the voice of a woman, accompanied by a stringed instrument, that moved the men. In the ninth century, an anonymous Silk Road poet recalled one such female voice, and his words, for Sevara Nazarkhan and her followers, carry meaning today. The poet wrote,

> On a carpet of colors sat the congregation
> with candles aloft and drumbeats of anticipation.
> They waited for her ... and in lovely ascent,
> lightly upon them, like a falling leaf she went –
> the singer from Tashkent.

> Her lily-colored raiment flowed,
> her braided hair with flowers showed.
> A crown atop her snow white face had little golden bells ...
> that whispered to the people through the air.

> A song she sang so rich and sweet
> once sung, the crowd flew to its feet;
> and thus, well pleased, the people withdrew
> into the clouds and the rain.

"We are part of the Silk Road," Sevara says. "We are in it. We live on it. It's not that we must reflect the Silk Road in our work. It just turns out that way. When I sing my songs, they are all segments along that road because these songs were sung by the people who traveled in the caravans. The songs made people happy, and encouraged them to travel farther along the road. And maybe because of that travelers were able to complete their journeys, to make it here to us in what is now Uzbekistan."

Sevara's musical trademark, and the backbone of her success, is the contemporary twist she gives to the traditions. Her desire is to take the musical sounds of the Silk Road and fuse them with the accoutrements of twenty-first century music. She sometimes embellishes the words of Uzbek poets with subtle electronic musical flourishes, producing a contemporary world music sound that clings tightly to the folk heritage. Other times, she mixes Uzbek verse with the intonation of modern pop, producing works that manage to sound like Central Asian rhythm and blues with dashes of rock and rap. She says that "black music" – American blues and jazz – is her favorite, but complains there is not much of an audience for it in Uzbekistan right now.

Sevara gestures to the engineer that she wants to sing another song. This one is also about love – *mukhabat* – but with words Sevara wrote herself. The song is fast paced and absolutely modern, underwritten by electronic rhythms and powered by Sevara's deeply resonant soprano voice. This is club music, music to dance to. It is a popular sound among Tashkent's young people. The verse, which she repeats over and over, goes, "Now this is no longer love."

Sevara sings on her feet, and the music buffets her body about. She juts her head forward here and there, then shifts it deftly side to side in time with the melody line. It is a traditional Uzbek woman's dance gesture. All the while, in counterpoint to that, she raises her arms and holds her elbows level with her shoulders. When the music skips into a little triplet of sound – boom-boom-boom – Sevara's elbows bounce – boom-boom-boom – to underscore the action. Her forearms are bent ninety degrees at the elbow, and both of her hands jab at the air, with index fingers pointed to emphasize the beat. It strikes me as an exotic mix of Central Asia and Harlem.

Sevara did not perform at Mama's Fun Pub when we went there together on that first night of Ramadan. Her energy instead was fixed on the dance floor. She hopped off the ground like a kangaroo. She plied the air with her arms, and her shoulders swayed and jiggled. She pranced about on one leg, and then on the other. Often she danced alone, lost in the crowd, enjoying the moment. During a break, I spotted her drinking a beer as she chatted with admirers.

Sevara was more conservatively apparelled than most of the other women there that evening. White jeans and a white blouse fully cloaked her body. Nobody could see her navel. But she was, still, most definitely a party girl, a woman, a Muslim, who knew how to have fun.

On the Saturday of the second week of Ramadan, Sevara suggested we visit a place called Zangi Ota. Located on the western outskirts of Tashkent, Zangi Ota is, for Uzbek Muslims, one of the country's holiest sites. A fourteenth-century mosque and a Muslim cemetery fill the grounds. The former was built, legend says, by Amir Timur – Tamerlane – Uzbekistan's national hero. It is the spot that local Muslims say they must visit before making the haj to Mecca. Sevara told me she had last been to Zangi Ota on the morning of the first day of Ramadan, the morning preceding the party at Mama's Fun Pub. "I come here often," she said. "This is a place where you can cleanse yourself. It is a place that will ease your troubles."

We went to Zangi Ota because I had asked Sevara to show me a place, in or around Tashkent, that best reflects the character of the Uzbek people. "Tashkent isn't really representative of Uzbekistan," she said. "You need to get out of the city."

En route to Zangi Ota, the police halted our car. Policemen are ubiquitous in Tashkent, and car stops not uncommon. At some places in the capital, officers line the streets fifty yards apart. It is the after-effect of the 1999 terrorist bombings. The public doesn't seem to mind the nuisance, for the city's streets are safe to walk on, even late at night.

A uniformed officer asked to see our documents.

"I'm Sevara Nazarkhan," Sevara told the policeman, hoping to talk her way out of the confrontation. The officer gazed at her blankly. Our driver exited the car and returned three minutes later.

"The cop rubbed his fingers together and demanded a bribe," the driver said. "I refused to pay. I bowed respectfully, told him we didn't break the law, and he finally said we could go."

Fifteen minutes later, we pulled up at Zangi Ota. It was a cold November morning, the temperature just above freezing. The grounds were mostly empty. Four beggar women sat on a curb in front of the mosque, huddled together shoulder to shoulder. "Salomalaykum," they said, holding out their palms. Sevara returned the greeting and gave them some money.

As we approached the mosque at Zangi Ota, a young Uzbek man walked up to Sevara, flashed her a toothy smile, and warmly shook her hand. The man wore a tebeteika and a long, black woolen coat. "This is Farkhad," Sevara said. "He works here. Nice to see you again, Farkhad." Farkhad smiled again and offered to be our guide. He led us first into the courtyard of the mosque.

The surrounding architecture is textbook Central Asian: an arched portal opens up into a colonnaded courtyard. In the center stands a brick tower from which the crier, or muezzin, makes the call to prayer. A small minaret caps the tower, and a handful of larger domes top the mosque's central building. The exterior and interior walls of the structure are laden with tilework: floral and abstract geometric designs set in shades of turquoise, purple, and brown, all delicately framed by Arabic calligraphy.

An anteroom set in the side of the mosque holds the tomb of the man named Zangi Ota. "He was a well-known cleric who passed down all of his knowledge to us," Sevara explained. "He was one of our great scholars, a great person who was also a poet. He constantly prayed, and it is said that if you come here to his grave you will find freedom."

Sevara entered the anteroom and approached a wooden gate that guarded the grave of Zangi Ota. She touched the gate with open palms and drew her hands down its wooden planks. She then cupped her hands like an open book, a traditional Muslim posture for prayer. She stood silently for a moment, then rubbed her face, indicating the moment of meditation had ended.

Back in the courtyard, to our right, a Muslim elder stood with an old Uzbek man. They hovered over a small hole dug into the ground. The elder held a dead chicken by the neck. "It is a sacrifice," Sevara said. "Come this way."

We walked to the rear of the mosque, which faced the adjoining cemetery. "Now we're going to the place that we think Amir Timur used to visit," Sevara said. On our left, a small alcove cut into the mosque's exterior wall. It was black as an unlit closet. Sevara led me in. In front of us rose three thick, ancient steps carved out of stone, leading to nowhere. The burrow was cold, and intimate. Our voices echoed, even when we whispered.

"Amir Timur is believed to have stood on this very spot," Sevara said softly. "Here he received his blessings. When he began his military campaigns he would come to pray for victory. He was very smart and very strong, and praying here reinforced those traits. So we come here to pray, too. I'll say a prayer for you now."

Sevara bent over and rested her palms on the top of one of the stairs. She closed her eyes and quietly prayed. When she finished, she again cleansed her face with her hands.

Our final stop that morning was a box-like mausoleum that stood in the middle of the cemetery. It housed the grave of Ambar-Bibi, one of Zangi Ota's wives, as well as the grave of Ambar-Bibi's daughter. We took off our shoes and walked inside.

The floor was a soft tapestry of red, gold, and blue carpet. Two tombs occupied the far corner. A rectangular stove lay just inside the entrance, covered with layers of blankets, like a tea cozy. "Please sit down on the ground," Sevara said. "Put your feet under the blankets and keep warm, but don't put them too far in. It's very hot."

I took a spot next to Ambar-Bibi's tomb, and rested my back against its marble facade. Sevara sat to my left. Opposite me sat an old Uzbek man in a black tebeteika with a prominent nose and a wispy snow-white beard that grew to a point six inches below his chin. He was an oksokol, a "man with white beard," one of Uzbek Islam's respected gerontocracy. The oksokol began to pray in a barely audible voice. Farkhad, who had joined us, took over the chanting after scarcely a minute.

Farkhad sang a melancholy prayer, a poem from the Qur'an. He punctuated the chant with trilled notes and ended his phrases with a bark of the voice, as if for emphasis. The prayer concluded anticlimactically, on a minor key, with a gently articulated note trailing off into the well of the mausoleum interior. "Rakhmat," Sevara said. "Thank you."

On the ride home, I asked Sevara why she believed Zangi Ota expressed the character of the Uzbek people. "There is a link to our ancestors there," she said. "Amir Timur came there himself. And any Uzbek can come there, be he poor, rich, ill, or the most contemporary man or woman. They all come because they can cleanse themselves though prayer. It is also a place where there is a direct connection to God. You can pray at home, of course, and I do. But there are distractions in the home. At Zangi Ota there are none. Only prayer. That is why the Uzbek people like the place so much."

"Is there a connection between this place and your music?" I asked.

"There is. Of course," she said. "There's a very close connection. When you sing you give voice to your inner emotions. And that is what you do in prayer. There is a certain karma at Zangi Ota. And this has helped me to develop, to move forward in my life."

"There is a big difference between Zangi Ota and Mama's Fun Pub," I noted.

"Naturally," Sevara replied. "Mama's Fun Pub is a place for entertainment. At Zangi Ota you come to rest your heart, to rest your soul, to free yourself from troubles."

"For a Muslim, can these places coexist?"

Sevara was silent for a moment. "That is a difficult question," she said. "I don't know whether the Qur'an permits entertainment. I think it says the more you suffer, the easier it will be for you in the afterlife. But, you know, the realists among us think differently. A realist wants to take in all he can from this life, all the happiness he can get, all the beauty and even entertainment. A realist faces a million obstacles in life and doesn't care whether he winds up in heaven or in hell. He doesn't know whether there even is an afterlife. Even the holy people, like those at Zangi Ota, cannot know for certain what the future will hold, because, having been the offspring of simple people, they are not absolutely holy. Even they can sin."

Sevara paused. "As for Mama's Fun Pub," she said, "I have a hard time answering your question. I need to read more, to live more in order to understand fully."

"This is a country filled with Muslims," I said. "I had thought Uzbekistan would be a rather conservative place. So Mama's Fun Pub surprised me. Those young women there, all so scantily clad, all that erotic dancing. How do you explain that? How does that square with Islam?"

"Those women, they look like Britney Spears, don't they?" Sevara said, smiling. "Look, I think we have taken everything bad from the West – from Western media and film – and we try to copy it, even to the extreme, as if we can do it one better. I'm not saying these girls you saw at Mama's Fun Pub are bad. They look at the world abroad and they think that by acting it out they are expressing freedom. They know they are young and pretty and they can get away with stuff without any worries. As you grow older and gain more experience, you change. I consider myself to be a bit conservative. And I relate to these young women with a smile. I don't criticize them. Today they go down one path. Tomorrow they may grow and choose another. This is the way people develop."

Back in Tashkent, Sevara and I parted. Off walked a woman who embodies the gist of what is post-communist Uzbekistan, or at least what the young in Uzbekistan aspire to be. Sevara is a Muslim who has managed to thrive in a secular Islamic world. She adheres to her religion with spiritual dexterity and gives voice to her country's traditions in an equally free-wheeling manner. She is apolitical but has maneuvered her way through a politically authoritarian environment – one that prohibits freedom of the press and billyclubs those who partake in free speech – to make it as a big-time entertainer. She sings what she wants in the manner she wants. Her recordings have landed on top of the musical hit charts – they do have them in Uzbekistan. In a country where poverty is widespread, Sevara travels and tours abroad and can afford to spend money in restaurants.

For those in the West for whom Islam has meant the Taliban and the veil, Sevara Nazarkhan represents a different paradigm. She is the familiar, moderate voice of a modern young profes-sional, a child of post-Soviet Central Asia – a child of Tamerlane – who can sing, dance, and drink and not lose sight of the fact that she also is a Muslim.

4

The Oldest Qur'an

In the old part of Tashkent, houses are made of straw and of clay, and the domes and minarets of aged mosques and madrassahs – religious schools – delineate the skyline. In Tashkent's old city, Uzbek, not Russian, is the language of the street, and women dress more modestly – more reverentially – than in the city center, where everyone speaks Russian, where Nike vies with French boutiques, where a post-independence spurt of construction – a paroxysm of glistening marble and gold-tinged glass – proclaims a wholly modern look. In the old town, you can feel a sense of history. Tradition reigns.

In the old part of Tashkent, in the anteroom of a sixteenth-century madrassah-turned-library, in a locked glass vault protected from the elements and kept at a constant seventy-two degrees Fahrenheit, sits the oldest Qur'an in the world.

It is, according to UNESCO, which has certified the manuscript and placed it on its "Memory of the World Register," the "earliest and definitive" existent written version of the wisdom of God as revealed to the Prophet Muhammad.[33]

The manuscript itself, visible behind the glass, is large, thick, and obviously brittle. To turn its pages – if one had the opportunity – would seem to risk the document's destruction. It is written in Kufi, the classic heavy and bold script of the ancient Islamic scribes. The parchment, when closed, is 24.4 inches long and 20.8 inches wide. In the vault the book rests open, its wings spread, revealing row after row of black-lettered calligraphy penned on animal skins, some 250 pages. A small slip of yellowed paper marks the pages that are stained in blood.

Therein begins the story of this Qur'an, which was penned in seventh-century Medina and which, inexplicably, found its way to Uzbekistan.

The Qur'an is the bible of Islam. Muslims believe its content was revealed to Muhammad over the course of twenty-three years, ending with his death in 632. Somewhat shorter than the New Testament, the Qur'an consists of 114 chapters, known as surahs, which spell out the fundamental theological precepts of Islam. "It is impossible to overemphasize the central position of the Qur'an in the elaboration of any Islamic doctrine," writes Huston Smith, a preeminent religious scholar. "With large portions memorized in childhood, it regulates the interpretation and evaluation of every event. It is a memorandum for the faithful, a reminder for daily doings, and a repository of revealed truth. It is a manual of definitions and guarantees, and at the same time a road map for the will. Finally, it is a collection of maxims to meditate on in private, deepening endlessly one's sense of the divine glory."[34]

Following Muhammad's death, three elected successors, called caliphs, sequentially assumed his position as Muslim leader. The third caliph, Othman, who was one of Muhammad's sons-in-law, sought to solidify his authority by issuing an official version of the Qur'an. He ordered the surahs gathered into one book (in Arabic, a *mushaf*), which he declared the standard Islamic text, superseding all others. In 656, Othman was assassinated while reading his Qur'an, known today as the Mushaf of Othman. The Caliph's blood still stains the manuscript, the tainted pages noted by that slip of yellowed paper. Othman's murder had long-lasting consequences: it "precipitated the deep Sunni–Shia schism which has divided the Muslim community since then."[35]

Tashkent is far from Medina, and Uzbekistan is not among the world's Islamic points of light. Officially atheist under communism, Uzbekistan today strives to impose a secularism that tolerates religion but keeps it in its place. It is a surprising and odd repository for the oldest Qur'an in the world.

There are a handful of accounts that purport to explain how the Qur'an of Othman made its way from Medina to the territory of present-day Uzbekistan. The journey has been the subject of scholarly investigation for more than a century, and the truth – whatever it is – remains, in the words of Boris Lunin, an Uzbek historian, an "open question."[36] UNESCO says all accounts are rooted in the popular tradition. It credits two renditions. Version one, it says, involves a relative of Caliph Othman, who purportedly brought the Qur'an to Central Asia during the period of internal disorders in Medina following Othman's assassination. Version two, according to UNESCO, centers on Tamerlane.[37] This story, Lunin maintains, is "the most likely and reliable."[38] Tamerlane conquered Iraq, and in the city of Basra, the story goes, he found the Qur'an of Othman, brought there by Othman's successor, who had made Iraq his base. From there, UNESCO says, Timur brought the manuscript to Samarkand, his seat of power. "It is well known," Lunin writes, "that Amir Timur related to everything concerning Islam with respect and concern, and that he took great care to preserve religious cultural artifacts."[39] Sufficient justification, in Lunin's view, to accept the Tamerlane connection as the most likely explanation of how the Qur'an of Othman wound up in Uzbekistan.

The Qur'an remained in Samarkand for centuries, ostensibly undisturbed, amidst Tamerlane's collection of books and artifacts. Lunin writes that in 1863 an adventuresome scholar from Hungary visited Timur's gravesite and discovered Othman's Qur'an for the non-Islamic world. The book was "resting on a dais" near Tamerlane's tomb.

At this point folklore gives way to fact. In the 1860s, the Russian empire was expanding into Central Asia. The Great Game was at its peak. In 1868, the army of the Russian Tsar, Alexander II, captured Samarkand. It was a critical victory for Russia in Central Asia. Peter Hopkirk, the preeminent chronicler of Moscow's campaign there, wrote that for the Russians the fall of Samarkand had a special significance: "For it was from here, nearly 500 years earlier, that the great Mongol commander Tamerlane had launched his fateful attack on Muscovy. The capture of [Samarkand], this legendary city, with its dazzling architectural splendors, including the tomb of Tamerlane himself, was seen as the settling of an ancient score."[40]

An ancient score, once settled, that yielded significant booty. According to Lunin, a general named Abramov laid claim to the Qur'an of Othman, which had been hidden in a Samarkand mosque. Abramov maintained that the local Islamic clerics voluntarily relinquished the manuscript to him because, in Abramov's words, "they said that nobody could read it and that it had no significance for Muslims." Lunin suggests Abramov was delusional in a self-serving, imperialist kind of way. Abramov more than likely forced the Samarkand clerics to give it up. If the locals considered the folio not valuable, Lunin asked, why would they have tried to conceal it from the invading Russian forces?[41]

Abramov's boss was the Governor General of all Russian forces in Central Asia, Konstantin P. Kaufman. Having learned that the Qur'an of Othman had fallen into Russian hands, Kaufman had it dispatched to St. Petersburg, the Russian capital, where it was deposited in the Imperial Public Library, and, at times, into the hands of imperial venture capitalists who made a killing on the sale of facsimile copies. One Uzbek scholar familiar with the Qur'an's history maintains that Kaufman himself profited from the sale of twenty-five such reproductions, which he is said to have purchased for fifty rubles each and sold for five hundred.[42]

In 1917, revolution hit Russia, first in February, when tsarist rule gave way to a moderate provisional government, then in October, when the Bolsheviks seized power. Lunin reports that in the days after the February uprising a group of revolutionary soldiers, who happened to be Muslim, were billeted in St. Petersburg, where they assaulted the Imperial Public Library in an unsuccessful effort to liberate the Qur'an of Othman.[43] The incident revealed pent-up anger among Russia's Muslim population over the theft of a holy relic, a sentiment that would soon demand the attention of the highest Kremlin authorities.

In the years following the October Revolution, Soviet power spread, in violent fits and starts but with eventual success, to the far reaches of the tsarist empire, including to Turkestan, the region that now includes Uzbekistan. Islamic leaders in Turkestan – and indeed in other Muslim-populated areas of the former Russian empire – viewed the Tsar's ouster as an opportunity to reclaim the Qur'an of Othman. Vladimir Ilich Lenin, the Bolshevik leader, faced the necessity of solidifying control over his newly acquired Muslim constituency. "What on earth can we do," Lenin asked, "with such peoples as the Kyrgyz, Uzbeks, Tajiks, and Turkmen, who up until now have been under the influence of their Mullahs?"[44]

Not being of a mind to let them be, Lenin instead imposed Soviet control by force and sought to assuage the Muslim population by returning the Qur'an to their fold. In December 1917, the Bolshevik government, in a conciliatory gesture, decided to send the ancient manuscript from St. Petersburg to a region called Bashkiria, to a city named Ufa, which since the eighteenth century had been the administrative center of Islamic life in Russia.

The decision did not please the Turkestan Muslims, who wanted to undo Kaufman's deed. They were determined to see the Qur'an of Othman return to the place it had resided since the reign of Tamerlane. Islamic clerics in Tashkent, Bukhara, and Samarkand allied with secular scholars – one of whom, a certain Professor Shmidt, was well connected in Moscow – to press the local communist authorities, as well as those in the Soviet capital, to order the Qur'an out of Ufa and back to Turkestan. All this unnerved the Tashkent communists. In August 1923, in a document marked "top secret," the Central Committee of the Turkestan Communist party resolved "to ask Moscow to block the return of the Qur'an to Tashkent." Its repatriation, the document maintained, would amount to "an anti-communist, anti-Soviet act, since conveying the Qur'an to the Islamic clergy would create a fetish for the strengthening of religious feelings among the Muslim masses in Turkestan, and would provide material for a spate of counter-revolutionary and anti-Soviet attacks by the clergy, which would utilize the Qur'an to enhance their power over the dark Muslim masses."[45]

The "dark Muslim masses," however, prevailed. Moscow, after a visit from Professor Shmidt, agreed to the repatriation. Murod Gulyamov, the Tashkent librarian charged with caring for the Qur'an of Othman, told me Lenin himself ordered the move.

"Do you happen to know whether Lenin ever saw the Qur'an?" I asked.

"The Qur'an of Othman? Of course he saw it," Gulyamov replied.

"Lenin saw it?"

"Yes."

"Tell me about that," I asked.

"We didn't witness what happened. History has written about it. There are books."

"Can you give me the details?" I asked. "When, why, how did Lenin see the Qur'an, and what did he have to say about it?"

"God knows about this. I don't," Gulyamov said.

The Qur'an of Othman came back to Turkestan on 26 August 1923. It was stored in a Tashkent museum in the Old City. As a condition of its return, the Qur'an was placed under continual armed guard[46] – in effect, under wraps – a safeguard that doubtless provided the local communist leadership some reassurance that the manuscript would not become a magnet for Islamic-led anti-Soviet intrigues.

Fig. 3. Abdulrashid Qori Bakhromov, Mufti of Uzbekistan.

In March 1989, at the height of the thaw known as "perestroika," the Communist Party of Uzbekistan transferred authority over the Qur'an of Othman from the State Historical Museum to the Uzbek Islamic Center in the Old City of Tashkent. At the time, Abdulrashid Qori Bakhromov was imam of the Tellya Sheikh Mosque, where many of Tashkent's devout regularly gathered for Friday prayers.

"People came from all over Uzbekistan to see the transfer," Bakhromov said. "They carried the Qur'an, passed it from hand to hand, lifting it above their heads. And they did so reverentially, with tears in their eyes, and they delivered it to our library."

"It was the first time I saw this Qur'an," Bakhromov recalled. "When it came into our library, I was shaken to the depths of my soul, because I had studied the Qur'an from beginning to end since my childhood, and because the Qur'an contains the words of Allah."

In 1997, the Uzbek government, which tightly controls religious affairs, promoted Bakhromov to Mufti, or chief spiritual leader, of Uzbekistan. He was also named Chairman of the Muslim Board of Uzbekistan, the government-controlled body responsible for administering Islam. Bakhromov, in effect, became President Karimov's point man for religion. One part of Bakhromov's portfolio is to explain government policy to the outside world. That is why he agreed to meet with me.

The administrative offices of the Muslim Board of Uzbekistan are located in the Barak Khan madrassah, an ornate building dating back to the sixteenth century which is situated across a narrow, dusty street from the Tellya Sheikh Mosque and the library housing the Qur'an of Othman. On the day I visited, a beggar woman plied the area, asking for handouts.

The entrance to the Mufti's office is inside the madrassah courtyard. A small reception area greets visitors, who are told to remove their shoes. Several men hover behind a desk, perusing a shiny new computer. Rolling across the monitor are verses from the Qur'an, complete with Arabic audio. It is a digital Qur'an, quite the foil for the nearby Othman manuscript.

A young man named Aziz – "I can't tell you my last name," he says – is the Mufti's assistant for international affairs. He leads me into the Mufti's office and introduces me to Bakhromov. "Please sit down," the Mufti says, and we settle into two couches beneath a lifesize-times-two portrait of President Karimov, which dominates the room.

The Mufti is an unimposing, slightly pudgy man who appears to be in his forties. He has the look of a scholar, with a soft, uncalloused handshake. He is modestly dressed in a white shirt and a green robe and slacks and he roams the room in white socks. On his head is a blue velvet tebeteika. A short, neatly trimmed beard peppered in gray covers a double chin. A squiggly scar cuts into the left side of his nose.

The Mufti leans back into his couch and begins to talk about Islam in Uzbekistan. As he speaks, his arms orchestrate, first right and then left. His eyes are mostly fixed on his hands, not on his visitor.

"I believe that our guest is familiar with our country," Bakhromov says. "Uzbekistan has given the Islamic world many great scholars, and, despite the fact Islam was born in Saudi Arabia, it has flourished here."

The Mufti explains that Muslims in Uzbekistan follow a liberal Sunni Islamic tradition known as Hanafism. "Nearly fifty per cent of the world's Muslims adhere to Hanafism," he says. "Hanafism promotes peace across the world, and rejects violence. What happened on September 11 was horrible. They showed it here on television. Criminals who take the blood of innocents in the name of Islam are not Muslims. The whole world knows that. Here we advocate tolerance among our own people, and towards other religions."

Tolerance was the issue I wanted to talk about. In the West, Uzbekistan is condemned for treating devout Muslims harshly. The subject even made the editorial page of the *New York Times*, which succinctly presented the case:[47]

> Uzbekistan is leading a regionwide crackdown on all forms of Islam that are not state-controlled – repression that is driving entire villages into opposition and forcing religion underground ...

The government has arrested thousands of religious Muslims and sentenced hundreds of them to long jail terms, even though they were not accused of violent acts. Thousands of villagers in Islamic areas have been forcibly resettled.

The *Times* described Karimov's policies as "crushing." "If a Taliban-style threat arises in Central Asia," the paper wrote, it will be because Karimov and like-minded Central Asian "dictatorships inadvertently helped to create it."

"You have heard the complaints," I said to the Mufti. "The American Congress, the State Department, they all say that it is difficult for religious Muslims to practice their faith here."

"This is a very interesting question," Bakhromov said, appearing absolutely unperturbed with the turn in our conversation. "Some people believe that in Uzbekistan it is impossible to study religion, to practice religion in your daily life. In fact this is not true. These rumors are disseminated by terrorists and extremists, people who envy our quiet life here."

"So how specifically do you respond to the allegations?" I asked.

"I say that over the thirteen years of Uzbekistan's independence there have been many changes: there used to be eighty mosques; now there are two thousand. There used to be two madrassahs; now there are ten. We have opened an Islamic institute. The Tashkent Islamic University has been working for five years now. Earlier, in Soviet times, only two or three people could make the pilgrimage to Mecca each year. Now we send four thousand people there annually for the haj."

Aziz, the Mufti's assistant, interrupted. "The number is actually closer to six thousand. Now, if you don't mind, the Mufti needs to go to the mosque to pray."

With the interview over, Aziz accompanied me outside. I expected to be reprimanded for raising the issue of human rights. I got something else instead.

"Something bothers me," he said. "I would like to visit America, but it is impossible to do so. The Mufti has been there twice, you know."

"Can't you get a tourist visa?" I asked.

"I have tried. The embassy won't give a visa to anybody. Look. You know me. I am an ordinary man, a religious man. Could you help me to get a visa, simply to look at America?"

"I'm afraid I won't be able to help you."

Aziz looked disappointed. "I don't understand. Why do the Americans give Uzbekistan such a difficult time? We have good relations. I don't know. You must think we all are terrorists."

The Mufti's defense of Islam got me to thinking about Sevara Nazarkhan and about other Muslim friends I had made. They all told me they felt free to practice their religion as they chose – they prayed five times a day, they read the Qur'an, the men went to the mosque. I wondered where the line was. What did somebody have to do to cross the line from permissible religious behavior to behavior that might get them into trouble with the Uzbek authorities? For an answer, I spoke with Allison Gill, a lawyer and researcher at the Tashkent office of Human Rights Watch.

I told her what the Mufti had said to me, about all the changes that have taken place since the fall of the Soviet Union.

"I'm not arguing that there hasn't been a change," Gill said. "Certainly I'm not arguing that. But just because the government doesn't repress some religious groups or some religious activity, it doesn't follow that everybody is free to practice as they choose.

The criminal codes very clearly criminalize peaceful, private religious activity that's protected by international human rights commitments that Uzbekistan has signed. So to your friends I would say, okay, try to get together in a group and study certain texts; or go out and tell other people about your faith as Allah commands. Or try to go to a mosque or follow a charismatic imam that isn't in a registered mosque." Do these things, Gill said, and more likely than not, "you might run afoul of the law."

"I think the line that you asked about is one that primarily involves state control," she said. "You've been here long enough to know that this is a highly controlled society, from the central government down to the mahalla neighborhood. There are all kinds of control systems. And with religion that's really no exception. The criminal codes prohibit private religious instruction; they prohibit proselytism. There are mosques, but they have to be registered by the state; imams have to have their sermons approved by the State Committee on Religious Affairs before they're allowed to preach them; in the legal codes there are restrictions on religious dress; you can wear a headscarf, but it can't be a religious hijab – it has to be an Uzbek flowered scarf and it has to be tied behind the head instead of under the chin.

"It seems to me that what it means to be an Uzbek fundamentally is a very, very narrow kind of conception. On the one hand, this is an incredibly charming and hospitable and interesting group of people in Uzbekistan. On the other hand, what it means to be a good Uzbek or an acceptable Uzbek citizen has a very narrow definition. You have to be Muslim, but you can't be too Muslim; you have to be an Uzbek Muslim; which I think draws on both Uzbek and Soviet traditions of being in an enforced secularized state."

Gill said that the Karimov regime does not tolerate threats to that secularized state and uses laws restricting religion to target anybody whose faith might unsettle the status quo. "Religious activity that's unsanctioned by the state is criminalized and opens people up to harassment," she said. "It is quite easy for the state to use these religious articles to go after anybody: you know, they plant a couple of leaflets on you, they drag you in and charge you with unconstitutional activities, and there you go. It's routine."

That trend began in earnest after the February 1999 bombings. It continues after 9/11, Gill said. The Karimov government wants "to be a big player in the war on terror. And they want to be able to justify their oppression at home." Devout Muslims, she said, are routinely called *vakhabisty* – Wahabists – the sect linked to al Qaeda. Thousands have been arrested over the years, but Gill said there is little or no evidence to link many of these people with violent extremism.

"It is easier to prosecute someone under the criminal code for religious violations if that person is a member of a so-called extremist or fundamentalist group," she said. "I think largely that's why the term *vakhabisty* is used here. But we've monitored trials where defendants have testified that they've never even heard of the term Wahabism until they've read it in their own indictments."

Gill told the story of one man who, at the end of his trial, said, "You've called me a wahabist, but *you've* made me into an enemy. I don't even know what that is. And you've beaten me so badly in your basements that I can't even live any more."

Gill said the defendant "pulled a razor blade out from between his teeth and lip and attempted to slash his wrists. But his codefendants restrained him and pulled him back. That's a very stark

Fig. 4. Mark Weil, director of the Ilkhom Theatre.

example of this term being implanted on a group of people who don't even know what it means."

The connection between Islam and terrorism bothered Mark Weil many years before 9/11. Weil is artistic director of the Ilkhom Theatre, an avant-garde playhouse in Tashkent that, since its founding in 1976, has been an island of creativity and freedom in an otherwise droll and authoritarian sea. Weil has also been concerned about the Qur'an – obsessed, really – an odd state of affairs for a Jewish intellectual, even a Jewish intellectual born and raised in Uzbekistan.

His interest in all this arose, by necessity he says, in the period immediately following Uzbekistan's independence in 1991.

Weil spoke to me in his office down the corridor from the theater's stage. He described his working quarters as "one big

Soviet antique" – there's an old Russian TV there, Soviet-era furniture, and the odd portrait of Lenin. The walls are covered with the kind of drab, floral wallpapering that mark any dwelling as of the Soviet era.

Weil was born in 1952. His hair, still intact, is graying. His face, soft and kind, exhibits a certain weariness from stress. He is dressed in a blue tee shirt and jeans. He speaks with candor, and no apparent fear, even though he knows he is being tape recorded. He says he won't sacrifice freedom for censorship.

In Soviet times, Weil's theater thrived, even in the face of communism. It was the dissident voice of a young generation whose fame and reputation and popularity grew so steadily that even the communist authorities would not touch it. There were attempts, Weil says, in the early years to stifle his activities. KGB threats and the like. But the theater became such a hit, both in Tashkent and among Moscow's influential circle of artistes, that it survived nonetheless.

"There was one really old man who supported us," Weil recalled, "an old communist who probably didn't understand what we were doing on stage. But he really believed that the new generation should do what it wants. When the people from the Communist Party of Uzbekistan asked him, 'How can you support them?' this old man said, 'I'll put my party card on the table, but you cannot touch them.' They backed down. 'You're too famous; you're an old communist,' they said. 'You saw Lenin and Stalin.' And he said, 'Yes, I saw Lenin and Stalin. And you can't touch me either.'"

The Ilkhom, from its inception, operated in a basement performance space near the center of Tashkent, on property owned by the Ministry of Tourism. It was, literally, underground theater.

The repertoire from the outset was provocative. Weil's first play, *Duck Hunting*, featured a hero who absolutely rejected communism. And this was in 1976, the height of the reign of Leonid Brezhnev, a Kremlin leader who tolerated little in the way of nonconformist thinking.

In the 1980s, with the death of Brezhnev and, eventually, Mikhail Gorbachev's assumption of power, the Ilkhom became, in Weil's words, "a symbol of perestroika." "It was our time. They loved us. We received a lot of prizes."

Then, in 1991, Gorbachev resigned and the USSR collapsed. For the Ilkhom, for Mark Weil, and for Uzbekistan, it was an especially uncertain time. "It was the beginning of the growth of nationalism in Uzbekistan, which," at least in Weil's perception, "identified itself with the extreme side of Islam." "Indeed," Weil said, "the new nationalists felt themselves to be a majority and they wanted to let the minority – the European or Russian-speaking population – know about that. I remember hordes of people who mainly traveled [to Tashkent] from the periphery, and they were protesting against the Russians. They were incredibly aggressive. Parents were scared to let their children play on the streets and in the playgrounds."

The Ilkhom became a target. "Passions had started to run high outside of our theater," Weil said. "Some nationalist-minded ruffians promised to burn the theater down after a show. Why? They just did not like the performance in principle: the artistic means we used."

The Ilkhom, Weil said, did not engage in self-censorship. All themes were open to scrutiny on its stage: homosexuality, nudity, free speech. "For the first time we heard the words: 'You live in a Muslim country, so please take the trouble of following our rules.'"

Weil said the "new nationalists began to feel that they should take out the Ilkhom … One day, the Minister of Tourism came by and said, 'Leave this place.' It was awful, because he sent workers; they destroyed our entire exhibition hall. It was like fascist methods. He took out our grand piano, old paintings. We were put on the street."

Weil said the people of Tashkent, back in the early years of independence, had a fervor that a decade-plus of Karimov's rule has stripped away. "So they protested. They wrote a letter to Karimov. Thousands and thousands signed it. Karimov hated any opposition, and at that time he wanted to represent to the world that he was a progressive. So the Minister of Tourism lost his job. He was fired."

And the Ilkhom survived and, eventually, prospered. It is the only independent theater in Uzbekistan, the only company that does not take money from the government. "It is a kind of agreement," Weil said. "They don't touch us, but they do not support us. They don't control us, and they don't really understand why the Ilkhom attracts so many people."

Mark Weil has never forgotten the turbulent events of the 1990s and in particular the rise of anti-Russian sentiment among Uzbekistan's Muslim majority. Years later, he remembers the anti-Russian protests; he remembers the apprehension, the anxiety on the streets. As an artist, he decided to confront his feelings. The result was a play called *Imitation of the Qur'an,* which is based on the work of the great Russian poet Aleksander Pushkin.

The play, which premiered in February 2002, is complicated, and purposefully so, for it follows a group of people who are searching for the meaning of the Qur'an. The main characters are shooting a film based on two of Pushkin's poems, *Podrazhaniia koranu* (*Imitation of the Qur'an*) and *Prorok* (*The Prophet*). The filmmaker encounters a dark cross-section of humanity as he does his work. A nightclub girl in a black bra who dances under a Muslim veil. A drug addict. A smoker who douses the cast with gasoline, then threatens to ignite them all. It is a vision of human depravity and weakness, whose players pursue redemption and peace in the surahs of the Qur'an.

"I made this play because I wanted to overcome my own personal fear of Islam," Weil said. "In the 1990s, all the people of Tashkent, particularly those of European descent, had to face the aggressive population of the fundamentalist Muslims who threatened all those who were not of their faith. So as you can see, the people of Uzbekistan were forced to face the issue of fanatical believers and realize its significance a decade before 9/11.

"It took some time for me to realize that what was to blame was not the Qur'an or Islam, but rather those who have attempted to use it for personal self-validation in an attempt to gain power. These people claim to be the only ones who have the right to understand and interpret the Qur'an to the world. As an artist, I could not agree with that. I think the Qur'an belongs to all of humanity, just like the Bible and Talmud. I began to search for material that could help me express my interest in this topic, which is where Pushkin comes in. Pushkin also believed that the Qur'an belonged to all of the people.

"As far as the production goes, we did not want to reproduce an Arabic world on our stage. We wanted to remain in the present, in a modern world. The actors are shooting a film, where they read [Pushkin's] poem, search for its meaning, find the meaning, lose it, accept it and refuse it over and over again, until these revelations push them to find their own path to finding God. So the main message I am trying to send in the play is that everyone has a right to interpret the Qur'an and to build their own understanding of it, despite their cultural, ethnic, or religious background."

In the official history of the Ilkhom Theatre, called *The Unknown Known Ilkhom,* Mark Weil wrote that he began working on *Imitation of the Qur'an* two years before 9/11. The terrorist attacks, he said, gave his play urgency and an edge. "It was probably destiny that the play would be in our repertoire," he said.

Back in 1976, when Weil founded his theater, he searched for a moniker that would work for an artistic endeavor in a Muslim country whose actors would be both Uzbek and Slavic. "The word 'Ilkhom' comes directly from the Qur'an," Weil said. "It means 'inspiration granted to earthly creators by Allah.'"

5

On Love

She is about twenty when we meet her. She works as a waitress in a little cafe in a suburb of Tashkent. And there is a quiet man who also works there who really likes her and pursues her. And one night he gets very drunk and attempts to physically abuse her, or maybe rape her. We don't know for sure. She manages to get away. He's startled at his own actions and runs off. They continue working together and they talk about that night, and he says, "I can't remember any of that." And he apologizes for it. And in that moment she falls in love with him.

She said that it's very odd. Her friends said it was madness to fall in love with someone who has tried to hurt you. But she couldn't describe it. She just fell in love with him.

They got along very happily. And they moved in together and had a fantastic time and it looked as if he was going to ask her to marry him. And he was making overtures to do so. And she had a guilty secret that she had to tell him – that she wasn't a virgin when she met him. And she thinks this will ruin everything. And she tells him. And he doesn't mind. "It's not something that's in my principles," he said. "Don't worry." And she's so happy.

A few months later they're invited to a party in the neighbor's upstairs flat. They go to the party, and she doesn't know quite what it is, but it seems that the neighbor, a woman, is behaving towards her husband in a way that neighbors shouldn't behave towards husbands of other people, as she puts it. And the music comes on, and the neighbor's friend is there, also a woman, and they're both recently divorced. And he's dancing with them. And he says to her, "You go on, go home. I'll be down in a minute."

"Well I did go home," she says. "I was an extraordinarily obedient wife. This man was everything to me. I even darned his socks. I did exactly as I was told. I was a very good and an obedient wife and that's the way I wanted to be.

"But he didn't come down. Forty minutes passed and my heart was pounding. So I ran upstairs and opened the door and they weren't kissing – if they were, I would have killed myself – but they were dancing in such an intimate way that was so provocative. I was like a tiger. I jumped on him and screamed and said, 'You must come home with me now!' And he looked at me like it was my fault, like I had done something wrong. And he took me downstairs and that's when something terrible started. He started to beat me. And he beat me so much I called out and screamed and my old neighbor next door heard and she came in before I passed out, and he ran out.

"When I came to, I was so badly beaten I couldn't walk. My face was so messed up – I thought I should invite a painter to paint my portrait because nobody would believe it. I couldn't call the police, *obviously, because the police would do to him what he had done to me. And I couldn't bear the idea that they would do that.*

"So I stayed in the house and he came back. And he looked after me. He brought me tea to drink which I had to drink through a straw because my face was so deformed. And I stayed in bed for two weeks and he had to carry me like a child and he was beautiful to me. And he apologized. And he took me out shopping when I could go out and he bought me clothes.

"But he was always jealous and he didn't want me to go out by myself and he didn't want me to work.

"And we're not together any more. And I really miss him."

The way Mick Gordon sees it, there is no better way to learn about a nation than to ask its people how they love. The thirty-two-year-old Belfast-born theater director had done so in Britain. "Tell me your love stories," he said to the people of London. Hundreds of interviews later, Gordon developed *Love's Works*, at England's prestigious Royal National Theatre Studio. It was staged at the Gate Theatre. The *Daily Telegraph* called the production "near-perfect as a piece of experimental theatre."

In 2003, three years later, the British Council, a government arts and culture organization, asked Gordon to come to Uzbekistan. The Council operates a center in Tashkent, evidence of Britain's longstanding interest in Central Asia.

Collaborate with the locals and make some theater, the Council said to Gordon. The result – *Pro Liubov'* (*On Love*) – premiered in May 2004 on the Ilkhom stage in Tashkent. It offered up a unique, unfiltered window into Uzbekistan.

"Love stories are interesting because they bring up a nation's culture," Gordon told me. "And in Uzbekistan they will bring us face to face with the religious difficulties or the potential racism that traditional families have; with the relationship of women to men, the position of women, the difficulty of being poor and of sustaining a family."

Gordon arrived in Tashkent in September 2003, armed with a handful of dictaphones and tapes. He set off for the Ferghana Valley, with several Ilkhom actors in tow. His initial objective was to query Uzbeks about the issue of freedom. "The subject is obviously an interesting one in Uzbekistan," he said. After contacting forty people, only three had anything to say. The rest were too scared to talk.

" 'Freedom' is a shrill word here," Gordon said in an interview at his Tashkent hotel. "People were amazingly nervous about talking about what freedom meant to them." The few who did reply "inevitably talked about having no money, and therefore not having any freedom."

Mark Weil, the Ilkhom Theatre director, urged Mick Gordon to persist. Freedom is the most important issue in Uzbekistan, Weil maintained. Work harder and you'll get people to open up.

But something else bothered Gordon. "I felt like I'm being supported by the British Council, an organization that I can't represent fully because its principles and the very great endeavors it undertakes are about colonialism still. And I feel uncomfortable with that. Being a Belfast boy myself, I thought: how patronizing actually to come and ask what does freedom mean to you? It's such a loaded question. It suggests that I have an answer to that and I'm free and you Uzbekis are not."

So Gordon sought safer ground and returned to the issue of love. More dictaphones arrived – twenty altogether – and the acting ensemble of the Ilkhom Theater, with recording devices in hand, were dispatched throughout Tashkent and the Ferghana Valley in search of love stories.

The process did not unfold entirely smoothly. Uzbekistan's authoritarian government does not condone freedom of speech. Recording devices are regarded with suspicion. The police confiscated several dictaphones and tapes. And they held one of the project's staff members for thirty-six hours, ostensibly for activity unrelated to tape recording.

Uzbek citizens, however – 552 of them – did want to talk about love. Mick Gordon made the transcripts of these interviews available to me.

[A man named Timur speaks:] Well, here is the story. I have a friend; his name is Sasha. He is a magnificent kind of a man. Indeed, when God created him he remembered how a true man should look. He is a talented sportsman. He is from a wealthy family. Everything is perfect. Everything is good. And wherever he would go, all the women were his. Because they were crazy about his looks, his smile, his skills in treating women.

So, I shall straightaway proceed to the love story. It was the birthday celebration of a friend that Sasha and I had in common. A mutual friend. It happened that Sasha was very busy at work and could not come to the celebration for even five minutes. But he called and wished a happy birthday. And our friend says to Sasha, "Listen to me, it is not a good idea. Today is my birthday. Please come at least for two or three minutes, drink a shot of vodka, and then you may leave. This is as it should be. Please come."

Sasha said, "All right. I will try to steal away for five minutes to drink to your health. But no more. Then I'll have to leave."

So Sasha comes to the birthday party. And I'll always remember what happened. Here comes Sasha, he brings some vodka, champagne, chocolate, and other necessary stuff. Then he says, "I congratulate you ... blah-blah-blah ..." and suddenly he freezes. Like a picture. It was as if there was a movie and it stopped running. He freezes and looks at this one girl. She was sitting somewhere off to the side, away, far away from our table. She was helping to serve up the food. She was a neighbor of my friend whose birthday we were celebrating.

She was nothing special. A common girl. She had neither a great figure nor beauty nor some super-intellectual mind. She was homely. Just your common girl. A usual little mouse. But she had the feeling of woman.

And as soon as Sasha looked at her he simply forgot about everything else. He took a seat near her. He had come for five minutes, but he stayed until the end. Then he volunteered to see her off. Her name was Katya.

She only lived next door, but he took two hours to see her off. They talked and talked and nobody knows what they talked about. In short, he fell in love with her. Fell in love up to his tonsils. And she fell in love with him. Romeo and Juliet paled by comparison.

But his parents were against it. Why? Well, he is from a wealthy family, and she was not. He was the favorite and only son. His father doted on him. His mother loved him to distraction. His parents tried to arrange a marriage for him. They brought him many girls. "You like her, don't you?" they'd say. "Why don't you marry her? She agrees. We can come to an agreement with her parents." He says, "No, she does not interest me."

When he introduced Katya to his parents, well, they were in shock. She was a nobody. An absolute nobody. In fact, a common orphan from a children's home. Her parents had died when she was a child. She had been brought up by her aunt, who was handicapped, an invalid. And Katya's family was poor. She worked as a nurse in some kindergarten. She was by no means thè girl they wanted their son to marry. But Sasha was determined. He said, "Either her or nobody!"

Finally, by the sheer force of his character, after insistence and persistence, Sasha got his way. His parents told him, "All right, we agree. If you think that she is the only and the unique one, God bless you – live with her." So they got married. And they lived together, Sasha and Katya. And everything was all right, everything was fine. Nothing out of the ordinary. His parents bought them a flat, and they lived fine.

Then, later on, it so happened that there was another celebration. Something for another of our common acquaintances. I only remember that some of us had a drop too much to drink. Sasha was smashed. He got into a fight with someone. Someone tore his jacket. He fell into a ditch and barfed. I was the only sober person there and I said, "Guys, we should take Sasha home." And that's what we did. But Sasha was totally out of it. He didn't even know where he was. It was three in the morning. He rang the bell. Katya opened the door. Katya had neither words of reproach nor words of blame. Nothing. She said, "My dear, you've come home? Well, thank God. You poor boy, you have drunk too much." No reproaches. No mockery. No screams. No female scandals, like "You drunk, what kind of condition are you in? Look at yourself – everything is dirty, what is it?" There was nothing of that! There was instead a lovely, kind smile, with no maliciousness. Simply a darling, lovely smile.

Well, we brought Sasha inside the house. We had to carry him because he couldn't walk. We brought him inside and suddenly at this *very moment something happened he didn't like. He did not like something in her smile. In short, he was drunk and he swung his arm and struck her with all his might. And he was a hulk of a man. Fortunately, since he was so soused, he hit her somewhere on her trunk or shoulder. But, naturally, she is something like half as heavy as he, and she flies away with a crash and crushes against the wall. We jump on Sasha and restrain him and say, "Are you out of your mind? Who are you hitting? What are you doing? You should be ashamed, and so on."*

Well, we take him to his bed, and he falls asleep. We apologize to Katya and leave.

And now I shall tell you what had happened afterwards, from Sasha's own words:

He wakes up in the morning. His head hurts. He has a terrible hangover. He feels badly. His mouth is dry, like dandruff. His eyes stick together. There's a ringing in his ears. His soul is not as it should be. His charm is switched off. His understanding and perception of life is absent.

The first thing that he sees – and what amazes him most of all – is that when he opens his eyes there is a chair standing near his bed, an ordinary banal chair. And on it are his clothes from the day before. They have been ironed, starched, in other words, absolutely cleaned. He gets up and realizes that he is clean, too, not dirty as he was yesterday, that all is normal, everything is all right.

He gets up and, having a headache, tries to understand what is what, where, how, and why? And in comes Katya, with no words of reproach, nothing like that, with no such phrases as "Yesterday you did so terrible things, blah-blah-blah. Whom I am married to? You alcoholic sot, sponger, and so on." Nothing was even close to that. Instead, there was a kind, loving smile that could warm a man's soul.

Katya says to him, "My darling, you probably have a headache. Here take a tablet. Or if you want – I bought some sour milk for you this morning." To go out at six in the morning to buy sour milk for your husband, well, this is something incredible. In addition to all that Katya says, "My darling if you want to have a little nip to help with your hangover – I have poured for you a hundred grams of vodka."

Sasha keeps silent, speaks nothing. Then she serves him breakfast, which was amazing. A European breakfast no less. He eats it and keeps silent. He thinks, "Anyway, some day she will dress my head on a frying pan." But No! There is an absolute silence in this respect. No reproaches. He is confused. He came home the night before. Went to bed. Got up in the morning to a loving wife. As if everything is all right. He tries to remember. Then he suddenly recalls that something is wrong. And he looks at Katya, who is wearing a short dressing gown and short sleeves. And he sees a huge bruise. And he says to her, "Listen, where did that come from?"

And Katya replies, "Oh, you know, can you imagine? When your friends brought you home they left it to me to drag you into bed. We fell down and I bruised myself on the floor."

He asks, "Are you sure?"

Katya answers, "Yes, yes, yes. Nothing terrible. You will not love me less for having the bruise, will you? It will anyway disappear after a while".

So he goes to work, and there he sees two of his colleagues who were among the people who had brought him home the night before. Naturally they told him what happened, and they laid into him for what he had done to his wife. "What are you doing? You should not drink at all! Who are you?" and so on and so forth.

The work day was coming to an end and he left work early so he could go to the marketplace, where he buys the biggest bouquet of flowers, so big that it does not even fit into a car. He comes home, and asks the taxi driver to help him to carry the flowers he has bought – well, his financial status allows him to do so. He brings the flowers in and puts them in front of her legs and begs her forgiveness. He says, "Put on your evening dress, we're going to go out together to a restaurant." They go to the restaurant, and he begs for forgiveness in front of everybody.

And since then Sasha may permit himself to drink one mug of beer at the most. And on rare occasions, on special holidays, birthdays of his friends or something like that, maybe a small shot of vodka. After that he overturns the wine glass and says, "That is all!" And since then I have been at their home many times and I have never seen, heard, or felt any misunderstandings between them. They have a really happy love. To tell you the truth, I suspect that this is one of those very rare cases where love is so real. It is really a masterpiece.

According to the advocacy group Human Rights Watch, domestic violence in Uzbekistan is widespread and represents a serious problem. "Research among a wide array of social scientists, government officials, domestic violence victims, police, and women's non-governmental activists … suggests that domestic violence against wives is common," the group reported. "A survey conducted by one government institution in the late 1990s revealed that over 60 per cent of female respondents considered domestic violence to be a 'normal situation.'" One government official, a woman, interviewed by Human Rights Watch said, "Women are guilty if their husbands hit them. If a man is angry, the woman should approach him to calm him down … Our men are hot-tempered. Men don't like it if women cross them. Therefore, in discussions we teach girls to take care of their husbands and prepare dinner on time … Men never beat for nothing."[48]

"Uzbekistan is a very macho society," Mick Gordon concluded. "Women are still very, very much second-class citizens. And the men are emasculated because society doesn't allow them freedom of speech or freedom to express their opinions or to be successful independently within the political system. So instead, they exercise their authority and control over their women."

Domestic violence was a common theme among the love stories Mick Gordon and his Ilkhom colleagues collected. It was extraordinary, Gordon said, that people were willing to speak out in a country where speaking out can have negative consequences. They wouldn't talk about freedom because freedom is political. But love, Gordon said, even domestic violence, is utterly personal. The women "had nothing left to lose," Gordon said. "And they go, 'Yes, I will tell you this story, and please do something about it. I've tried. I've failed. It's pointless.'"

Often the abuse involved mothers-in-law mistreating their sons' spouse. Sometime the violence was between husband and wife, or girlfriend and boyfriend. One such tale – told at the opening of this chapter – was used in the stage production *On Love*. The audience gasped at the depiction of abuse. Other stories, even more deeply troubling, were not brought to the stage. Gordon abstained because he did not want anybody to get into trouble.

"I know that I censored some stories," Gordon said. "We were invited to a center that looks after young brides who were abused by their husbands' family – used as slaves, and also used sexually. And they tried to commit suicide by setting themselves on fire, because that is accepted, that does not bar your way to heaven. Obviously, they've been unsuccessful because they're still alive and this center in Samarkand cares for them. And we didn't use a story, which we got through a lawyer, of a woman whose husband had left her. He was an alcoholic. He left her and she couldn't support her five children. They were dying of malnutrition slowly. She then poisoned her five children and set herself on fire. She was unsuccessful and was tried and given life imprisonment."

The organization Minnesota Advocates for Human Rights has written that self-immolation among women in Uzbekistan is "increasing." In a report entitled *Domestic Violence in Uzbekistan*, the group cited an Uzbek journalist who said "it was not uncommon in the past for women to douse themselves with kerosene and set themselves on fire, especially in the highly traditional Ferghana Valley." The journalist told the group "that in the past, 30 to 50 cases a year were recorded and that this type of suicide is now on the rise." Another Uzbek source, an activist in a health NGO, told Minnesota Advocates "it was 'fashionable,'" and that "self-immolation increases the more people talk about it."[49]

"We didn't present those stories," Mick Gordon said, "because I was not certain that if somebody wanted to find out where the stories had come from I could protect the person who told the story and who gathered the story. So I said we're not going to perform these stories. I'm not prepared to take the risk. It's easy to go into countries and be provocative and basically fuck off back home, leaving other people to pick up the pieces. I was concerned that that wouldn't happen."

My name is Olga. I am thirty years old. I love money and I am not ashamed of saying so. My love for money can be seen from my relation to it. Yes! I love it! I love to earn money, love to count, and love to spend. I work as an accountant, naturally, and I think that money does everything in this world. Everything depends on it. Literally in all spheres of life you can use cash. I think I can buy love for money, I can buy a title, I can even buy an education.

Ah, don't feel sorry for me. Don't look at me funny. Money is power! Love for money! I do not believe in love at first sight, or that there is some sublime and pure love. I think that everything depends on the brutish attraction between the sexes, and therefore you can buy short-term pleasure and get it. What is the point of suffering for love when essentially you can buy it? A boyfriend will always be with me and will never leave me while I have money, while I have a car, a house, and everything pleasurable, while I can pay for pleasure. Yes! One can say that this is short term. But I will always earn money; I will always have money.

Money gives you freedom. If you have cash, if you have dollars, euros – then you are a free person. You can travel, see the world. And of course you can take someone with you. You can enjoy yourself and see things you would never see if you were living, say, in poverty.

Yes, I love these crackling papers, clinking coins. They give real happiness and they give me freedom.

You ask about the movies? I like it when the hero goes on some kind of adventure looking for treasure. Or steals someone's savings from their bank account. This is real love! This is real pleasure! Do love money. It will bring you happiness.

[A boy's voice:] My name is Stas. I am eleven. I like pets. I have a dog, and two hamsters. Their names are Homa and Petya, and the dog is called Grunya. I love them very much. I look after them, clean after them, and love them. They bring more gladness and harmony to my house. I like squeezing them, playing with them. My dog, Grunya, runs very fast. I can throw her a stick and she will bring it back straight away. And my hamster can do different stunts on the wheel.

They are very good at that. I also like dumplings, cheese, and pizza. This is all. Bye!

[A girl's voice, speaking in a kindergarten:] My name is Ira. Seriozha kissed me yesterday and now I don't know whether I will have a baby or not. But my girlfriend told me that I may, well, get pregnant. I'm scared. I don't know how I will feel when pregnant. My mother will drive me out of home probably. I love Seriozha and he loves me.

Mick Gordon says that love in Uzbekistan pretty much resembles love in the West, at least as he knows it. There are variations, he says, to be sure. In London, people spoke with more sophistication about love, infusing their stories with the vocabulary of psychology, "and what that lets you know is that there is a lot of leisure time in London, people have time to think about their relationships and their feelings, and that many people have been educated within a society that takes psychology seriously … That didn't happen at all in Uzbekistan. There was no theorizing on that scale."

Gordon said people were having extramarital affairs "left, right, and center" in the stories he was told in both London and Tashkent. He recalled the story of an ostensibly happily married couple in Uzbekistan who ran into each other at a sexually transmitted disease clinic, a scenario that would be equally plausible in Great Britain. But often, in Uzbekistan, the spouses were fixed up, their marriages arranged. "It was the usual Uzbeki story: the lady would say, 'Here's the husband my family found for me, and I married that man; and here is my true love, who is married to somebody else.' "

But Gordon concluded, after immersing himself in five-hundred-plus love stories from Uzbekistan and hundreds more from England, that love is one of those universal human emotions that plays itself out uniformly wherever you are. "And that love is, in its intensity, a disease. You're in love, you're in a heightened state, a state of dis-ease."

This story happened with my friend. He was very much in love with one girl, Uzbek, who was religious. She was Muslim, she learned Qur'an, she studied, and was, on the face of it, a kind, decent, good, very beautiful girl. He loved her very much and was always after her. But, since she was religious, he was afraid to come close to her, to look at her too intently, let alone to touch her hand or kiss her. Such a thing never happened. The girl had no father. There was a mother. There was a brother. They all said how good she was.

In the evenings she would come outside, in her long dress, head-scarf on her head. She would go somewhere, but nobody ever saw when she would come back, and, truly speaking, no one paid any attention to it. It seemed strange to this guy, who wondered why and where she went. He loved her and wanted to know about her more, because he wanted to marry her,

He himself also was Uzbek, with strict manners in his family. They were not doubting that she was decent, but they shared his desire to know a little bit more about her. So he started to follow her. He walked behind her, so that she did not notice.

One evening, this girl left her house, dressed as always in her long dress. She walked a long, long time and approached some strange nine-floor building and went into the doorway. And after a period of some time, a completely different girl exited the building. She was in a short skirt, high heels, and all covered with make-up. He did not pay attention to this girl. He waited instead for his beloved. He waited, waited, waited, waited for his precious one to come out. But she never did. So he went away.

The next day the same thing happened. His beloved left her home dressed in the usual Muslim manner, walked into that building, and never came out. When he saw the other girl leave the building, he went inside and searched all the floors for his beloved, but did not find her.

The next day, when the same thing happened again, he decided to go after that girl who was in the skirt. The girl caught a taxi. He went after her. Her car stopped close to some nightclub, and that girl came out and went inside. He followed.

It was obvious that she was a frequent visitor there, because she was greeting people, she had a lot of acquaintances, she kissed almost everyone there on their cheeks. After some time he saw this girl was dancing a striptease. And then she started walking on the tables in a kind of strange dance. Eventually, she approached his table, and they glanced at one another. And it was a great horror for him when he recognized in those eyes his girl, just that same girl, that same religious girl, whom he was planning to marry. Of course, once she saw him, she just blasted, and quickly ran to the backstage, or wherever she was running. He, of course, went crazy. He drank a lot and sat outside near the doorway, leaning on a tree, crying. He later went to her house and spat in her face. Just like that. And he went away.

And it was sort of difficult for him afterward, and he suffered for a very long time. He could not understand why everything happened the way it did, why this masquerade was needed. Basically he still loved her. He loved her not because she was religious. He just loved her and that's that.

Well, that guy eventually married a Russian girl, a simple pretty lady. At first his family would not accept her, because she was Russian and they were Uzbeks. But he reminded his family of that other, religious Uzbek girl, and what had happened with her. "There was your Uzbek lady!" he said. "Religious and so on, and look what happened!"

And in general he lives quite normally now with this new girl of his. But, for some reason, he can't let go of his beloved in the skirt. He asks us all the time, "Where is she? What's happening to her? How is she doing?" We heard she moved abroad. Travels. Dances. Earns money. And he still loves her sincerely. He remembers her a lot. It is a huge pain for him. Such is love.

Mick Gordon says that of all the love stories he collected in Uzbekistan, one in particular stood out, told by a seventy-year-old Uzbek man. It is not that the story itself was particularly compelling, Gordon said. In fact, most of the stories the Ilkhom actors gathered on dictaphones were fairly mundane and predictable. "When I first saw her I liked the way she looked." "We met in the park by the statue." Stories like that.

But this septuagenarian had a special, blunt wisdom to convey. He was, Gordon said, fantastically sagacious.

The man was asked if he had ever been in love.

"Love?" the man replied. "No, no. Never experienced it. Don't have any time for it."

"So we asked him whether he was married," Gordon continued. "'Yeah,' he said, 'I'm married.' 'What about children? You don't have any of those then?' 'Oh yes,' he said. 'I've got six. But this has no connection with love. I've always been just too busy working.'"

Gordon found that age bequeaths wisdom among the elderly in both Uzbekistan and England. "There were great lessons from the grandparents we interviewed, people who had lived long enough to get through everything and had experienced things and saw it all in their children. Their lessons were: "Look: unfortunately – lucky you – you'll fall in love. Well done. Hard luck. At the end of the day you'll realize that companionship wins out over passion. But you just don't know that when you're young."

She is a nineteen-year-old girl from Tashkent and she knows exactly what she wants. She sees across the room the man of her dreams. And she gets to know him. Things are going fantastically well. He's buying her flowers. He's buying her perfume. He's buying her small gifts and tokens of affection. They're from the right families. It is everything in her mind that she'd want a husband, boyfriend, father of her children-to-be. And she decides that "This will be my husband. We're going to get married." She decides this way before he's even aware.

Then she makes what she describes as a mistake, because she tells her best friend about this man. Now her best friend is, I wouldn't say loose, but she's entertained a lot of fellows. "And she doesn't take love as seriously as me," she says. "And when I introduce my best friend to my boyfriend, she looked like the cat who wanted the cream. She licked her lips. And my boyfriend, of course, he was a young man of normal sexual libido. He finds somebody who behaves in so obviously a crude sexual way interesting, as men do who have normal sexual libidos. And suddenly he stopped giving me flowers and he didn't call for me as much and my friend stopped coming over. And I heard from other friends that they were seeing each other behind my back. This is when I remembered what my granny had taught me – and thank you, granny, for teaching me to fight for my love.

"My boyfriend was still seeing me so I knew he wasn't in love with this girl so much as to dump me. So I thought, I won't cause a big drama about it. I will be clever and I will fight for my love as my

granny had taught me. So I changed ten thousand soum [one thousand soum equals approximately one US dollar] *into the smallest denomination of notes that I could – five soum, ten, twenty-five, fifty, one hundred. And I wrote this message on each of the notes: I said, 'If you want a good time, call me.' And I wrote my best friend's telephone number down and her name. And then I went shopping.*

"I went to the bazaar and I went to the local newspaper stand and went on the metro and I went on the busses and I went to the delicatessen and I went everywhere and it was the best shopping trip I ever had. And, funnily enough, in a few days my plan started to work. My friend's mobile telephone started ringing. And my boyfriend, who was with her on occasions, took the phone and wanted to know what all these men were doing calling my best friend. It must have affected her, because I noticed that she got fairly pale looking and she lost a lot of weight during that period. And sure enough, my boyfriend thought, 'I don't want to be associated with a woman like this.'

"Well, my story has a happy ending. We're going to get married. My parents are organizing everything."

6

The Horseman

Rustam Vladimirovich Samibekov, eighty-one, stiffened his slight frame – he was five foot four on a good day – stuck out his chest, and scowled at the four-legged animal that stood before him.

"Piligrim was very poorly raised," Samibekov complained. A horse trainer for more than half a century, Samibekov had no patience for equine imperfection. Any steed who misbehaved in front of Rustam Vladimirovich would get a swift smack in the face. Piligrim doubtless knew that.

"He was a pitiful colt," Samibekov said. "I knew Piligrim's father. I trained him with my own hands. And Piligrim's grandfather was a magnificent horse, a beauty, simply outstanding, a horse worthy of a tsar. But this one, he had a poor education. He wasn't trained properly. He never raced. So this horse is really only half-developed."

Fig. 5. Rustam Vladimirovich Samibekov, the horseman.

It was a shame, Samibekov said, that Piligrim was such a fail-ure, for Piligrim was a pure-bred, one of no more than a dozen or so horses in Uzbekistan that belong to a class known as the Akhal-Teke. The Akhal-Teke is also called the "Turkmen" horse – most of the breed now resides in neighboring Turkmenistan. For horse enthusiasts, it is the jewel of the stable. It is a horse with uncom-mon strength and stamina. A horse that once, literally, aroused empires and shaped history.

"It is an ancient breed," Samibekov said. "Its skin and bones are taut, with little excess flesh. In biology, a lean and slender consti-tution means strength. In this breed you will find endurance and power. He has a very distinctive exterior – a long neck, set very high, and this allows the horse to raise its center of gravity, enabling it to surge forward or fall back, as need be. This makes the Akhal-Teke very nimble, like a cat."

Samibekov himself was sprightly for an octogenarian. Elfish in appearance, he had twinkling eyes and a face that appeared younger than its years. When he spoke, he did so with enthusiasm, eloquently, with rising and falling intonation that gave his speech an orchestral quality. This was an exuberant man who relished each thought and each word. When he moved, he did so with determination. He scurried around the farm and stables of the Tashkent Hippodrome like a bullet train, albeit an aged one, tending to his horses.

"I don't ride anymore," he said. "Gave it up when I was seventy. I figured that if I fell at that age I'd break something that would never mend and I'd wither away into an ignominious death. If I were to die an old man on the battlefield, in a cavalry attack, that would be something different. I'd take at least five or six men down with me. But to perish because of some shitty two-bit fall – that would be disgraceful and degrading."

Samibekov is half-Uzbek and half-Russian. He traces his roots to the Ferghana Valley, where his father was born. Ferghana is the most soil-rich, population-dense, and poorest region of Uzbekistan. It has been the scene of violent protests against the regime of President Karimov and is thought to be a breeding ground for Islamic extremism. It was once, way back when, a breeding ground for the Akhal-Teke.

Samibekov recalled the story. Of how, in the second century B.C., at the time of the Han dynasty, a powerful Chinese emperor by the name of Wu-ti sent an emissary to Ferghana in search of a political alliance. The alliance never happened, but the emissary brought back word of a magnificent "heavenly horse" that he had found there, a horse that was extraordinarily swift and untiring, a horse that could outrace a falcon, a horse the Emperor could use to bolster his cavalry, a horse so wonderful and mystical that it sweated blood. A Chinese poet later wrote,

The Ferghana horse is gamed among nomad breeds.
Lean in build, like the point of a lance;
Two ears sharp as bamboo spikes;
Four hoofs light as though born of the wind.
Heading away across the endless spaces,
Truly, you may entrust him with your life.

Wu-ti resolved to purchase these horses. He dispatched another ambassador, laden with gold, back to Ferghana to do the deal. The ambassador was murdered and the gold confiscated. Wu-ti was enraged. He ordered six thousand horsemen and thousands of foot soldiers to assault Ferghana to take the horses by force. The campaign ended in defeat. A second attack followed several years later, a serious, Normandy-like invasion by an army of sixty thousand men, thirty thousand horses, 100,000 head of cattle and thousands of donkeys and camels. This operation succeeded. Wu-ti's general was presented with ten of the heavenly horses and several thousand regular steeds. Since that time, the Akhal-Teke has been bred in China.

"Yes, they sweated blood," Samibekov said. "But it is not what it appears to be. That is legend. These horses were light skinned, the color of a morning sunrise. They had a very tender constitution and very, very tender skin. Their blood flowed just beneath the surface of their skin, and when the horse became agitated and its blood flow increased, the horse took on a reddish color. That's why they were said to sweat blood."

Scientists have found another explanation. The rivers of the Ferghana region carry a parasite that horses ingest while drinking. The parasite subsequently breaks through the horses' skin, causing bleeding.

Centuries after the Chinese moved heaven and earth to seize the celestial horses, the Akhal-Teke moved the Russians. It was 1881, Samibekov said. The Tsar's army, under the leadership of General Mikhail Skobelev, defeated the Turkmen army at an outpost called Geok-Tepe, a victory that eventually would lead to the incorporation of present-day Turkmenistan into the Russian empire. Skobelev's victory was notorious, and was condemned by the world because Russian troops massacred thousands of women and children. What interested Skobelev, Samibekov said, were the Turkmen horses.

"He was amazed with the speed and galloping abilities of the Akhal-Teke, with the bearing of its neck, with its muscular body and long slender legs. To Skobelev this was a gazelle of a horse, an antelope. He summoned some of the Turkmen prisoners and, through an interpreter, asked, 'What kind of horse is this? What kind of breed?' They replied, 'This is our breed.' 'And who are you?' Skobelev asked. 'Bil akhal teke,' they said. 'We are the people of the billy-goat.'"

"*Teke* means 'billy-goat' in the Turkic language," Samibekov explained. "Men of the Turkmen tribes wore long, classic beards – goatees – without moustaches. The beard was seen as a sign of prosperity. For that reason they were called *akhal teke* – the tribe of *teke*, or the tribe of the billy-goat. So that's why, in response to Skobelev, they identified themselves as the Akhal-teke people. And that is why Skobelev called the Turkmen horse the Akhal-Teke. This was a secondary name for the breed, born from Skobelev's nimble tongue. To this day, in Afghanistan, in Iraq, in Iran, in Syria, the Turkmen horse is known by another name, as *nissai.*"

Samibekov said the Akhal-Teke seared the imagination of the Russian military and stuck there for years after Skobelev's time. It was 1935, Samibekov said, and Josef Stalin was the dictator in Moscow. Like Wu-ti, the Chinese emperor, Stalin got wind of the Akhal-Teke and wanted them for his own. What transpired, Samibekov said, was a long march as amazing, or more so, than Mao's.

"The Turkmen wanted to please Stalin," Samibekov said. It was a troubled time, the height of the purges. Mollifying Stalin seemed to make sense. "So they organized a caravan of sixty stallions, Akhal-Teke, and these horses rode all the way to Moscow."

The journey covered eighty-four days and more than 2,500 miles, from Ashqabad, the Turkmen capital, to the seat of Soviet power. At one point in the expedition, the horses and riders traversed 225 miles of the Karakum desert in three days with almost no water. Desert temperatures hit nearly 150°F. They traveled mostly in the dark.

"The riders entered Moscow wearing tall sheepskin hats and red military robes," Samibekov said. "They were received with great fanfare. Stalin wasn't there to greet them. But his generals, Budennyi and Voroshilov, were." Stalin and his men took the best of the lot, the rest of the horses being deposited in Russian training schools and breeding farms.

Years later, in 1970, Soviet leader Leonid Brezhnev traveled to Turkmenistan, where Samibekov worked at the time as a horse trainer. Brezhnev came looking for horses, and Samibekov himself helped the Kremlin chief pick out an Akhal-Teke. "He chose a golden-cream-colored steed," Samibekov said. "I can't recall the horse's name."

Amazingly, the marathon trek from Ashqabad to Moscow was repeated in 1988. One Akhal-Teke expert has written, "This extreme long distance trek served to put the world, (most importantly, Russian officials), on notice that the Akhal-Teke was a rare and valuable breed of horse worthy of preservation and devotion to keep pure. In addition, it was pointed out that the Akhal-Teke could provide refinement, stamina and athletic ability to crosses with other breeds of horses."[50]

Rustam Vladimirovich Samibekov was never a communist. He never held a party card. But he did study Marxism-Leninism – "conscientiously," he noted – and he did believe in socialism.

Despite the Great Terror. "My father was murdered in the Stalinist camps. He was arrested in 1938, and I never saw him after that."

"Why was he arrested?" I asked.

"We have a saying here about Stalin: he developed diarrhea one day, and the next day it was you who was soiled and flushed down the toilet as an anti-Soviet agitator."

In 2002, a Museum for the Victims of Repression opened in Tashkent. It pays homage to Uzbeks who died at the hands of the Soviets and of the imperial Russians before them. The blue-domed shrine memorializes those "who gave their lives for freedom of the Motherland during nearly 130 years under the colonial yoke." The museum was built on an execution burial ground – on Amir Timur Street across the way from the Yunusabad tennis complex – where, in 1937 and 1938, the bones and bodies of some thirteen thousand Uzbeks, shot by Stalin's police, were buried.

"I fought in Stalin's army," Samibekov recalled. "I was in the infantry. They sent everyone who was suspect into the infantry – and I was suspect because of my father. They figured the foot soldiers would die off first. It was a good filter to get rid of undesirables.

"I saw combat. I was wounded. A spinal injury. And, you know, riding horses somehow fixed my spine up just fine. There wasn't a horse that could get the best of me."

After the war, Samibekov returned to Uzbekistan and began a short-lived career as a singer. "I have a good voice. I'm a baritone, and I was a soloist in the radio committee's ensemble. Then I entered the Musical Conservatory and studied to be an opera singer. Eventually, my love for horses got the better of me."

Then, amidst the dust and hay of the horse stable we happened to be conversing in, Rustam Vladimirovich Samibekov let loose a song, a cappella:

Smartly adorned with a cap on my head
I ride the gallop of the steed ...
Past my mischievous, beautiful lady
Let her recall me like this, indeed.

Ah, how I gallop and fly through the night
Past apple blossoms and roses
Sing my steed, sing at the sight
Of my beautiful girl as she poses.

Rustam Vladimirovich Samibekov has written that "the horse and the dog are genuine creatures of nature. These true friends and servants of man bring forth in one's heart deep sympathy and love. Possessed of these emotions, I have given up my life to the cult of the horse, rejecting earthly wealth, completely devoting myself to working with them, studying their lives, their demands and individual characteristics. It is difficult to explain, even to myself, the passion, joy and, sometimes, the despair that I feel about them."

Desperation came in buckets to the stables of Rustam Samibekov during the late 1950s. "I was living and working in Turkmenistan at the time," he said "I was a master trainer." Then came the order from Moscow: kill all the horses.

"Nikita Sergeevich Khrushchev was leading the country, and he decided to slaughter all the horses – dogs and cats, too – in order to catch up with the United States in meat production." Thousands and thousands of animals were liquidated, their meat consumed at home and sold abroad. The Akhal-Teke were not exempt.

"More than fifty per cent of the Akhal-Teke in Turkmenistan were eaten," Samibekov said. "It was an act of sabotage. It was savagery."

Samibekov fled Turkmenistan, with seven Akhal-Teke in tow. He went back to Uzbekistan, but the local authorities, implementing Khrushchev's orders, would not allow him to train the steeds. "So I left and went to the Caucasus, where I was received warmly, and I had all my horses sent there."

Among them was a horse named Sardar. He was among the best Akhal-Teke Samibekov ever encountered. "Sardar means 'General.' He was a marvelous jumper. I trained him for the steeplechase, the big steeplechase in Baku – six kilometers, thirty very difficult barriers. And his training was going wonderfully. I figured he would beat the best previously recorded time by twenty seconds.

"But here in Central Asia there is a very dangerous tick that can give a horse malaria. And this tick bit my Sardar. The illness was horrible. The blood dies of asphyxia. The eyes turn a terrible red. The urine is bloody. Temperatures of forty-two degrees [Celsius; 108°F]. A horse collapses within three or four days. And Sardar fell victim to this tick-borne disease ten days before the race. I grieved horribly."

Samibekov paused, experiencing again the loss.

"Rustam Vladimirovich," I said, "you speak about these horses as if they were your children."

"Yes, yes. I'm a natural born trainer. I have a decent apartment in Tashkent, and, wherever I have lived, I have had apartments. But I forsake them and choose to live instead with the horses."

Samibekov's apartment in Tashkent was near the city center. But for most of the year he and his eighty-year-old wife, Anastasiia, lived in a room in a barn at the city's Hippodrome. It was a small hovel with two beds, a stone's throw from the stables.

"A trainer must be near his horses all the time," Samibekov said. "Only then can he feel their needs, their appetites, their behaviors. Only then. Therefore, I have lived my entire life along-side my horses, and they, of course, are all my children. I deliver them. I care for them from birth. They are all my children, and when they die I cry, I cry bitterly, I cry ceaselessly."

Rustam Samibekov died on 22 March 2003. One of his stable hands told me, "He was here that morning, training the horses, cleaning them. He went home, took a bath, and died."

Samibekov is buried in a plot across a dusty road from his stables. Sculpted into his gray marble tombstone is a portrait of this horseman of Uzbekistan, his chest covered with World War II medals. Behind Samibekov's likeness the head of a horse is etched. A memorial has been set up to honor Samibekov at his stable. A sign reads, "How can we live without him?"

7

Cotton

In the annals of American history, few agricultural crops have had as much impact on the nation as cotton. "King Cotton," as it was called, did much to define the southern way of life. Even northerners can hum the tune of the song that begins, "Way down yonder in the land of cotton."

Look away – a world away – to Central Asia, and there is another land – Uzbekistan – where cotton has had an equally defining role. Uzbekistan is the world's fourth-largest producer of cotton and second-largest exporter.[51] The crop is a critical prop to Uzbekistan's economy. And it is central to the country's identity.

Turn back the clock thirty years, to a time when Uzbekistan was still part of the Soviet Union, and place yourself just about anywhere: in Tashkent in the northwest; in Ferghana in the east; in Termez in the south; in the westernmost province of

Karakalpakstan. It is the mid-1970s. A hot September or October morning. Clear skies. Temperature 105 °F. Harvest time.

Turn on the radio. A song comes on, generated by the state propaganda machine. It is a bright and happy melody, uplifting in a subtle kind of way, sung by a chorus of eager men and women. It is a song heard so often that, decades later, children of the era can recall it as adults. The song is intended to bolster the spirits and spark the work ethic of tens of thousands of Uzbeks – men, women and children – who were to flood the fields and labor the day away collecting what was and remains the single most important commodity in Uzbekistan. Cotton is arguably the principal legacy of communist rule there. It was Joseph Stalin who turned the country into one large cotton plantation to supply the rest of the Soviet Union. Since independence in 1991, Uzbekistan's cotton crop has remained the government's primary source of income. It accounts for more than forty per cent of the country's exports.[52] In Uzbekistan, cotton is called "white gold."

Cotton is native to Uzbekistan. But were it not for a bit of *American* history, cotton and Uzbekistan might not have been so closely linked. In the years before the US Civil War, the US south was the principal cotton supplier to the Russian empire. Once the fighting began in America, exports from the Confederacy were cut off. The Tsar had to look elsewhere, and he set his sights – and soldiers and agricultural experts – on what now is Uzbekistan.

One of the varieties of cotton seed used in Uzbekistan today comes from the United States. Its name is "Dixie."

If you walk in a cotton field at harvest time, as I once did, you will wade through a sea of brittle, knee-high stalks. Balls of cotton the size of a baby's fist flower from the branches. It has been said that Uzbekistan is two-thirds desert and one-third cotton. That is

Fig. 6. Khamza Mansurov, director of the Tinchlik cotton fields.

an exaggeration. But the crop is grown on almost half the land under cultivation. And owing to the lack of wealth to support mechanization, eighty-six per cent is harvested by hand.[53]

Khamza Mansurov is director of the Tinchlik cotton fields, about ten miles west of Tashkent, on the road to Samarkand. I visited him one October morning.

Mansurov is forty years old. He has a ruddy complexion and a thick tuft of curly black hair. His hands are rough. He has been working the fields for nearly twenty years. He says for him cotton is like a lover. He can never take his mind off it, especially at harvest time. It gives him passion. And, he says, it can give him heartache.

Mansurov supervises a workforce of three hundred. Surrounding him in the fields are some men, but mostly women, kerchiefs covering their heads and faces, shielding them against the mid-day sun. These are families, Mansurov says, who have leased the land, something not allowed in Soviet times. These people have a stake in the harvest. The more cotton they collect, the more money they make. Under the Soviets, Mansurov says, the state kept everything.

Uzbekistan's most famous communist leader was Sharaf Rashidov. He led Uzbekistan for most of the 1960s, 1970s and 1980s. While in Tashkent, I was able to procure a bit of history: an old, tinny recording of a Rashidov speech. He was speaking in 1977, on the occasion of Moscow awarding Uzbekistan the "Order of the Red Banner." In his remarks, Rashidov praised that year's cotton harvest as a "triumphant success ... achieved by the strong hands of Uzbek men and the tender hands of Uzbek women."

What Rashidov did not say was that the success was a product of his imagination. From 1976 through 1985 Uzbek party officials overstated cotton yields by millions of tons, and the excess crop payments received from Moscow were embezzled by the country's political elite.

It was the Soviet reformist Mikhail Gorbachev who eventually cracked down on the Uzbek leadership. Hundreds of Uzbek officials were arrested and, by many accounts, overzealously prosecuted. Rashidov was disgraced. Today in Uzbekistan, this so-called "cotton affair" is seen as an act of Soviet repression, the most infamous episode in the country's long association with cotton. Rashidov has been rehabilitated as a national hero of sorts for having defended Uzbekistan's interests against the Kremlin.

The present Uzbek government, like its Soviet predecessor, centrally manages the nation's cotton production and continues the Soviet practice of setting ambitious annual targets for cotton harvests. The pressure to produce is enormous. That is the heartache Mansurov spoke of.

At harvest time, the country literally mobilizes in a fourth-quarter rally to snatch up every single blooming bud of cotton. Across Uzbekistan, police cars lead caravans of busses along the country's roads. The busses are followed by flat-bed trucks stuffed with rickety bed frames and mattresses. The convoys are carrying students and soldiers into rural areas to pick clean the cotton fields. It is mandatory work. According to the US State Department, compulsory mobilization of children, mostly in rural areas, also occurs during the cotton-picking season. Human-rights activists say that sometimes the police surround cotton fields to ensure that the workers aren't slacking off, or skimming off yields to sell on the black market.

Matilda Bogner, a researcher at the Tashkent office of Human Rights Watch, explained that forced child labor is pro-hibited under international law. "Every year during the cotton-picking season various parts of the population are sent out to pick cotton and that includes children in Uzbekistan. They are forced to pick cotton whether they want to or not, and it happens through local government authorities who approach the heads of the schools, who then tell the teachers to take certain classes out to pick cotton. My understanding is that there's a shortage of labor for picking cotton. It's not a very popular activity. And so children are called upon to fill the gap in terms of labor."

Bogner said the children are taken away from their parents "for a period of several weeks to a couple of months." "They will usually live in conditions which are not very adequate, especially towards the end of the season. It's already November and starts to get cold. There's often not adequate heating, or adequate food given to the children."

Bogner said the children's ages can range from six or seven years up to eighteen. "Usually it's ten-, eleven-, and twelve-year-olds and higher who are taken out to pick cotton."

Maria Shurochenko, twenty-three, worked the cotton fields north of Samarkand when she was a nineteen-year-old university student. "It was obligatory," she told me. "If we would not go we were excluded from the university."

Shurochenko said the work was hard. "We were working all day long under the direct sun. The daily norm, we had to pick about forty kilograms of cotton [eighty-eight pounds], which is a huge amount. This is very difficult for people who did not grow up in rural areas. And the food was awful. We were hungry almost all days, and our parents had to bring some food for us."

In the autumn of 2004, the Institute for War and Peace Reporting (IWPR) released a report on child labor and the cotton harvest. The report, based on extensive field research, accompanied a photo exhibition of children harvesting cotton. Entitled "The Cost of Uzbek White Gold," the photos, taken by German photojournalist Thomas Grabka, were displayed at the Ilkhom Theatre in Tashkent. You can see some of the photos, as well as excerpts from the report, at the IWPR's Central Asian website (<http://www.iwpr.net/centasia_index1.html>).

The fact of the exhibition was remarkable, in that public discussion of child labor in Uzbekistan is taboo. Grabka's photos starkly depicted pint-sized, stony-faced boys and girls at work on the harvest. One especially powerful picture showed an empty classroom, with a picture of President Islam Karimov on the wall glaring over rows of vacant desks. The students who normally occupied those desks had been forced to abandon them for the cotton fields.

The IWPR report covered the harvest of 2004. It presented a harsh portrait. Here is what the IWPR said about living conditions:

Housing for the young labourers is often primitive. Many stay in farm storehouses, without glass in the windows or doors to keep out the cold. Some are housed in school classrooms, crammed into a single, unheated room with up to thirty-five others. Dirty drinking water is a serious problem. Uzbek human rights organizations say many are forced to drink untreated water from wells. But water brought in for the children is little better as it is often unpurified and kept in filthy containers contaminated with mud and worms. Many have no access to bathing facilities for the length of their stay in the cotton fields. Their staple diet is macaroni, bread and sweet tea with little meat available. How much food they get depends on what they earn, usually about 20–25 soums [two US cents] per kilogramme gathered. Local headmasters are on hand to make sure the children pick the required daily amount, which changes according to the state of the harvest.

The report also addressed health problems:

Not surprisingly, many children end the cotton campaign in poor health and unable to make up the weeks they've missed at school. Some suffer from colds, and there were reports this season of two children falling sick with appendicitis. Tragically, some never return. A Samarkand human rights organization has confirmed the deaths of eight children and university students while picking cotton over the past two years. Those in charge of the harvest, desperate to hit Tashkent production targets, are reluctant to send the children to hospital because they need their labour to hit the state-imposed quotas. A lack of the most basic medical equipment only adds to the health risk for the youngsters. To gain their child an exemption from picking, wealthy families will often bribe local health authorities for a certificate of poor health. This option, of course, is far out of the reach of ordinary Uzbeks.

There is another side to the cotton harvest in Uzbekistan. At least for some of the older students, and for some of their parents, the picking of cotton is considered a matter of national pride, a proving ground, and something of an adventure.

In the rural village of Hisarak, about an hour's drive from Tashkent, a thirty-nine-year-old mother named Mamlakat spoke of her sixteen-year-old daughter's time in the cotton fields. It was a good thing for her daughter to do, Mamlakat told me. "I want my girl to be independent. She will soon marry and move to another home. By being sent to the cotton fields she experiences the difficulties of life, and that will prepare her for the future."

At the Tinchlik cotton fields run by Khamza Mansurov, I met three students, all nineteen-year-old women, who had been working the fields for twenty days. It is not possible to gauge whether they spoke honestly to a foreign reporter, but they said they did not mind the work. Sevara, a medical student, described it as "interesting and pleasurable." She said the girls were housed in a nearby dormitory, where the food was hot and there was a disco in the evenings. Her friend Anfisa said she enjoyed laboring in the fields because she could endlessly chat with her friends.

Kevin Griffith, an American Peace Corps volunteer, found similar sentiments when he worked for two days with Uzbek students in a cotton field called "Kaitmas," northeast of Tashkent. Griffith said *kaitmas*, an Uzbek word, means "the place of no return."

Griffith said many of the students' parents and siblings had picked cotton, so it seemed natural to the students that they would do so too. "And the fact that they were teenagers," he added, "meant that they were able to get away from mom and dad. And at night there were discos. There were interactions between genders that might not go on back home, such as dancing and maybe adolescent flirting. But at the same time, in the field, they weren't happy with the work they were doing. They were picking cotton and were sweaty and dirty."

"Cotton is a tradition," Griffith said. "The host family mother that I live with now picked cotton when she was a child. And when I looked through her photo album I saw a picture of her and her friends with cotton sacks wrapped around their backs and smiling faces. And I think when the students head out to the cotton fields now, they don't consider it labor entirely. I think they also consider it a tradition, part of what other family members and Uzbeks have had to go through in the past to keep the economy alive. And in a way, they are doing their part to enhance national pride and national unity. And they are contributing to their economy by picking this cotton which is not able to be picked in any other manner."

The nature of that contribution to the economy has been a point of contention for Uzbekistan's farmers, who are obligated to sell most of the cotton they harvest to the government at a price that is one-quarter of what the government will earn when it sells the cotton in the foreign marketplace. David Pearce, head of the World Bank's office in Tashkent, said the government profits big-time. "The government deliberately uses the differential in the two prices, the low price it pays to farmers and the international price it obtains from exporting cotton, to subsidize what it considers other priority investments elsewhere in the economy, some of which we see around the city of Tashkent in terms of modern, urban infrastructure and so on."

Pearce said the government's policy of buying low and selling high is hurting Uzbekistan's farmers, who are deprived of wealth and of incentives to increase cotton yields. But this harm is nothing when compared with the damage that cotton has done to the environment in Uzbekistan. Meet Ajinyaz Reimov, a twenty-nine-year-old environmentalist.

"Only recently I learned that I have stones in my kidney, and it's due to the very salty content of the drinking water in Karakalpakstan," Reimov said.

Karakalpakstan is Uzbekistan's westernmost province, and Reimov grew up there. He spent a lifetime drinking tainted water. "When you drink water with salty content it gets filtered in your kidney and some of the pieces are large enough not to go when you urinate."

Nearly everyone has kidney stones in Karakalpakstan, Reimov added. High rates of infant mortality also plague the region, and hepatitis, typhoid, and cancer are widespread. All can be linked to the ecological catastrophe caused by cotton. David Pearce said the environment in Uzbekistan began to deteriorate in Stalin's time. "The decision by the Soviet Union to make Uzbekistan the center for production of cotton – given the desert nature of the topography here – led to a massive investment in the fifties, sixties, and seventies in water irrigation infrastructure."

What the Soviets did, Pearce explained, was to take water – lots of water – from Uzbekistan's two main rivers (the Syr Darya and Amu Darya) and divert it into a maze of cotton-field irrigation canals. Massive doses of pesticides and fertilizers compounded the situation by poisoning the irrigation waters, which eventually ran off into the two rivers. The result has been what some have described as "ecocide." The Aral Sea, which once fed off those two rivers, has shrunk by some two-thirds. Winds rake up toxic salt from the exposed sea bed and rain it down on thousands and thousands of acres of adjacent farmland, mostly in Karakalpakstan.

David Pearce said that in post-Soviet Uzbekistan things are

beginning to get better. The Aral Sea is shrinking at a less dramatic rate. And the farmlands are breathing somewhat easier. "There is less fertilizer," he said, "less pesticides, certainly of the old variety available, and so to this extent the level of annual damage created by the improper use of those things has stabilized and may have improved actually."

Sadulah Khokimov, a journalist and poet, is glad of that, but laments the Soviet Union's role in ruining the land of Uzbekistan. "The Soviets robbed us," he said. "Brezhnev used to say 'Golden hands harvest white gold.' But it was the Soviets who got rich, not us."

He recounted a relevant anecdote, told in Uzbekistan, that dates back to Soviet times: "A collective farm director was having bad headaches, so a doctor opened up his skull in surgery. And instead of gray matter, instead of a brain, the doctor found cotton. The doctor got scared and quickly closed up the skull. And he didn't tell the farm director what he had discovered inside his head. Four or five years passed, and the doctor met with the director again. The doctor asked, 'So how are you? Is everything okay?' 'Yeah, everything is okay,' the director said. And the doctor thought, 'How can that be? He's got cotton in his head instead of brains.' So the doctor decided to tell the director what he had discovered. 'Remember when I operated on your head? I found cotton inside your skull instead of brains.' And the director said, 'Why do I need brains in my head when the Soviet communist bosses are there to make all the decisions?'"

"We have been harvesting cotton in Uzbekistan for more than two thousand years," Khokimov said. Uzbekistan's people survived the Soviets, and the Uzbek land will survive as well. "It is blessed," he said, "and nature will bless it with sunny skies to give the farmer a bountiful harvest for all eternity."

Part Two

Part Two

A Dispatch about Life in Contemporary Uzbekistan

Let me begin with a true story. It is about Uzbekistan and Winnie-the-Pooh.

I lived in Uzbekistan for the better part of three-and-a-half-years. My wife, Eriko (a United Nations diplomat), son Ariel, and daughter Katrina (who was born half-way through our tenure in Tashkent) shared the experience. So did our Russian nanny, who, as you shall see, is the link to A. A. Milne's literary icon.

Some background: When it came time to leave Uzbekistan, we needed to ensure that the Uzbek authorities would allow us to send everything home, back to the United States, without interference. Uzbekistan has laws prohibiting the export of certain cultural artifacts – archeological gems from Tamerlane's time, and the like – and imposes fees on the shipment of other works of art. Our personal effects had to be vetted before departure.

Among the belongings we had acquired in Tashkent was a piano and an oil painting. The piano, built in 1964, was made in East Germany. It had somehow found its way to Uzbekistan, which at the time was part of the Soviet Union and therefore a socialist comrade of the communist-run German Democratic Republic. The oil painting was the product of a local Tashkent artist.

Since both items could be considered valuable objets d'art, we were required to ask the Ministry of Culture for permission to send them abroad. The moving company we hired to ship our household consignment was responsible for making the arrangements.

After our things had been packed up, a representative of the moving company visited my wife at her office. He presented her with documents from the Ministry of Culture indicating official permission had been granted to export *four* artifacts – one piano and *three* works of art – each considered to be of historic and artistic significance to the Republic of Uzbekistan, and each therefore requiring an export fee.

"Three paintings?" my wife asked. "But we only have one."

Inasmuch as we had to pay for each item, there was reasonable cause for concern.

The man from the moving company, a thirty-something Uzbek national, reached into his briefcase and produced photographs he had taken of the three canvases at issue. One was of the abovementioned oil painting. The second and third were of paintings that had hung in our son's bedroom. Our nanny, a talented amateur artist, had sketched them for Ariel as gifts. One portrait bore the exact likeness of Winnie-the-Pooh. The other was a big, blue representation of Thomas the Tank Engine, a popular children's character from Britain.

The Ministry of Culture had officially registered Winnie-the-Pooh and Thomas, too, as national treasures of Uzbekistan.

To understand Uzbekistan is to understand that Uzbekistan has an Alice-in-Wonderland underbelly. It is a country where a nanny's portrait of Winnie-the-Pooh can become a national treasure. It is a country where inexplicable and arbitrary behavior – on the part of the Ministry of Culture or of anyone else – is commonplace, indeed the norm. It is a country without a commonly understood legal culture, a country whose citizens regularly and wantonly drive on the wrong side of the road, a country whose people look out for themselves and not for the rule of law. It is a country where the police are pretty much everywhere and are perceived to be protecting their own interests rather than those of the public. It is economically a poor country, a very poor country, a country of traders where bargaining and bribery are national commodities, a country where pretty much anything, or anyone, can be bought. It is a country where fear – sometimes subtle, sometimes not – is central to the way of life: fear of the government and of the police, fear of speaking freely, fear of sticking out, fear of terrorist attacks.

I kept a diary and reporter's notebook when I lived in Uzbekistan, and also transcribed many an interview. Here are some relevant entries. My intention is to answer the question everyone who has never been to Uzbekistan asks me: What is it like to live there?

THE LOCKSMITH

4 August 2001 – After nearly twenty-four hours on the road from New York, we moved into our temporary Tashkent residence, an apartment on Sharof Rashidov Street near the Ministry of

Interior. We'll be here a few weeks until our regular house is ready. We arrived to see a locksmith working on the apartment's door. A security guard from Eriko's office explained that the old lock had a problem.

The locksmith's name was Naril, a thirty-year-old ethnic Tatar with a ruddy complexion. We spoke. He mentioned, without my even asking, that things had gotten worse in Uzbekistan over the past ten years, since the breakup of the Soviet Union. "Such are things with our leader, Karimov," he said. Then, looking over his shoulder, he added, "I had better not talk, since the walls have ears."

Naril was having a lot of trouble replacing the lock. He had been asked by Eriko's office to complete his work in advance of our arrival, but had failed to do so. He was agitated. The old lock was just too stubborn. It stuck. Simply ate up keys. And wouldn't surrender to Naril. It was an original Soviet model, many, many decades old, and was one of the last items not yet renovated in the flat.

Naril finally managed to extract the old lock from the door's wooden frame, but was struggling to fit a replacement lock into the gap. When he announced he had finally completed the work, we decided to test the new device. Eriko, Naril, and two-year-old Ariel stayed inside the apartment. I stepped into the exterior hallway and closed the door, which Eriko proceeded to lock from within. The lock seemed to work just fine. But it would not unlock. Push, pull, shove, kick. Nothing worked. The door would not open. My family was stuck in a fortress with a locksmith, and I was standing in an unlighted hallway which was growing blacker by the minute as the night set in.

Ariel started to cry. "Daddy? Daddy? I want daddy to come inside the house!"

Naril was getting quite nervous about the whole thing "It's not my fault," he said through the door. "It's this Soviet equipment. It's very unpredictable and difficult to replace."

Nice metaphor, I thought, to describe Uzbekistan's efforts to reconstruct itself from the rubble of the Soviet collapse.

Finally, after forty-five minutes of herculean shoulder work, Naril released the door.

It was late. We were tired. I told Naril to finish the rest of the job in the morning. He agreed, and added I should use the still-viable bolt lock for overnight security.

"Let me try it," I said, closing the door and twisting the bolt. It didn't engage, so I pushed the door harder to get it to close completely.

Click. The new, defective lock engaged.

"Don't do that!" Naril pleaded. Too late. I had unintentionally restored the door to its formerly irrevocably stuck position. My family was captive inside again, with Naril outside in the unlit corridor with me.

Naril fumbled to remove the wooden door frame in an effort to get at the stuck-again lock. He pried planks of wood off their moorings with a screwdriver. No luck.

I told a somewhat frantic Eriko through the bolted door to call her office. Naril was now really worried. "They'll have me fired from my job," he said. "I need this job. I must get inside your apartment. I'm going to go to your neighbor's flat and climb out their window." He added, quite sincerely and without the slightest bit of braggadocio, "I may be risking my life."

Five minutes later, Naril was inside our apartment, speaking to me from the other side of the door. He had gotten permission to enter the apartment below ours, climbed though an open window onto a ledge, and three stories above ground winnowed his way to our dining-room window and pulled himself into our flat.

After some more shoulderwork, he pulled open the door.

Naril was drenched in sweat. He extracted all remnants of the new lock and said he would return the next day at 10:00 A.M. to finish the job.

"Nice to have met you," I said.

"You too," he replied, "although I think you would have preferred if you hadn't made my acquaintance."

"No, no, not at all," I said. We shook hands and he left.

Naril showed up the next morning at 9:15 A.M. He came with a lock consultant. They studied the door and said they needed to get some new parts. Naril said he would return at 6:00 P.M. He didn't. We had to find another locksmith to complete the job.

THE TERRORIST CAT

22 August 2001 – Something – or somebody – walked on the roof of our new home last night. I had just fallen asleep. Eriko was still awake. The lights in the living room were on. At 11:30 P.M., Eriko woke me up.

"Rob, come here," she said. Her voice had an uncommon undertone of urgency. I followed her from the bedroom into the living room. "Listen," she whispered. "I think somebody is upstairs."

I was incredulous at first. I listened. And I heard what sounded like footsteps coming from above. A heavy sound moving from one end of the house to the other. It had a metallic quality to it. And there was some scraping. And it didn't stop, as you might expect some harmless, ubiquitous house sound to stop. The noise was real, and a wave of adrenaline rolled through me.

I was scared. As foreigners, we had been warned that we might be targeted, either by crooks or by terrorists. Uzbekistan has its share of both.

Eriko and I stood motionless and listened. The footsteps continued. Neither of us knew what to do. Eriko grabbed her walkie-talkie, which had been supplied by the United Nations security team for emergency operations. "Stay down here," she said.

Eriko walked up the stairs to the second floor, which was dark. The first-floor switch for the second-floor lights had failed to work.

"It never worked," I said in an effort to calm the situation.

"Is anybody here?" Eriko asked. An odd question under odd circumstances, as if a terrorist intruder or a common thief would respond in the affirmative.

Nobody was upstairs. How, in fact, could someone be there? We lived in a citadel. A jail with a marble facade. Bars covered all the first-story windows. The house was protected with layers of locked and double-locked security doors. The UN wanted its folks to live in secure locations.

Eriko came back downstairs. "What should we do?" she asked. The noise on the roof, which had stopped, had been real, not imagined. We both had heard it. Could it have been some sort of animal? Too loud for a cat or a squirrel. Are there squirrels in Uzbekistan? It surely sounded human.

I put on some jeans and a tee shirt (I had heretofore been walking around in underpants), grabbed the keys, and went outside to turn on the lights in our courtyard. Once they were on, Eriko ventured out. It was an uncommonly cool evening, after a daytime high of ninety-five degrees Fahrenheit.

We both looked up at the roof, trying to discern something that could explain what had happened. We couldn't see a thing. We returned inside.

"Should I call Vlad?" Eriko asked. Vlad was with the UN security team.

"I don't know," I said, stupidly. "You're the one who has been briefed on security issues."

"I think we should call him," she said. Eriko dug up his business card, which was conveniently located in her purse.

She dialed.

A woman answered the phone. His wife.

"Can I speak with Vlad please? This is Eriko from the office." Vlad came to the phone. "Vlad, this is Eriko. Please talk with my husband."

Vlad didn't speak English. And Eriko's Russian was weak.

"This is Robert," I said in Russian. "Sorry to call you so late, but about ten minutes ago Eriko and I heard footsteps on our roof. I turned on the lights in the courtyard but we couldn't see anything."

"What's happening now?" he asked.

"Nothing," I said. "Things are quiet now."

"We'll be right over," Vlad said. The marines were on the way.

Fifteen minutes later a UN van pulled up. Vlad and Aziz, the chief UN driver, rang the bell. I went outside to let them in. Access to the house was through the courtyard, which was fronted by an exterior security gate.

At that moment the telephone rang. Eriko answered. A Russian-speaking woman asked to speak to somebody. After hearing Eriko's voice, she hung up. Earlier that evening the phone had rung numerous times – three or four – and nobody had been on the line. The same thing had happened during the day. Ring ring.

"Hello." Hang up. We figured it was the hiccuping of the totally screwed-up local phone network. Or harassment sponsored by the Ministry of Interior.

I explained again to Vlad and Aziz what had happened. And I told them about the phone calls. Vlad was alarmed by the calls. "How many? When?" he asked. "Who was on the other end of the line? Whom did they ask to speak with?"

"I thought these calls were just the result of the bad phone system," I said. "Is this unusual?"

"Yes," Vlad said. "Sometimes people call to see if anybody is home, and then hang up if someone answers. You should get caller ID if this continues."

Vlad and Aziz also questioned Eriko, who told them what she had heard. "At first I thought it was a cat," she said, "but the sound was too loud. It was definitely human. I thought it might be a construction worker." There had been construction work behind our house earlier in the evening.

Aziz climbed up the iron grate that covered the kitchen windows. The kitchen is a one-story extension to the two-story house. He peered over the roof. "At this level the kitchen roof abuts the neighboring home," he said. "But your second-story roof stands alone above everything."

He came down. It was 12:30 A.M. Vlad and Aziz left to survey the neighborhood. "Don't worry, Eriko," Aziz said. "We are here. Everything will be okay." They returned after five minutes. "Everything is quiet," Vlad said. "We can get you a guard tonight. One of us will stay. Then if you want we can arrange for a permanent guard tomorrow. Eriko, your boss has two guards who work from 8:00 P.M. to 7:00 A.M. each day. He wasn't able to sleep at night before the guards came. Now everything is fine."

I looked up at the second-story roof, trying to figure out what might have happened. "How could anyone have gotten onto the roof?" I asked.

"Robert, this is Uzbekistan," Aziz said. "This is not Europe. This is Uzbekistan." He paused to emphasize his point. "This is Uzbekistan."

Vlad spent the night in the courtyard. Eriko quickly fell asleep. I lay in bed, pondering the implications – if any – of what had happened. I felt insecure. Every little house noise doubled in its capacity to menace. After an hour – it was now 2:00 A.M. – I went into Ariel's room, adjoining ours. He had slept through the whole thing. I climbed into his bed and lay down next to him. For some reason, being next to my two-and-a-half-year-old son made me feel safe.

Ariel thrashed around in his sleep, as was his fashion. I didn't sleep at all that night.

Eriko said that by the time she got to work the next day everybody in her office had heard about our "security incident." That's what they called it. A "security incident." Tanya, Eriko's twenty-three-year-old assistant, said a drug addict had probably climbed onto the roof of our home. According to Tanya, Tashkent is filled with desperate addicts who will do crazy things – like climbing onto roofs – to steal money. Tanya said not long ago a drug addict had assaulted her house. The man hid in her garage all night long, and in the morning attacked her grandmother. Only the grandmother's screams forced the addict to flee.

Later the next day, at 4:30 P.M., Vlad and Aziz came back to our house to check on the roof. They had borrowed a ladder from our landlords, Rustam and Vasiliya, an Uzbek couple who lived across the street. Vlad climbed onto the roof and walked across its length. Eriko and I listened in the living room. The sound was identical to the one we had heard the night before. Vlad came back down. "Any trace of anything?" I asked. "No," he said. "The roof is clean."

Vlad returned the ladder to Vasilia, who was standing outside. I approached her.

"So you heard what happened last night?"

"Yes," she said. "We were out late at a restaurant and came home after 10:30. We were up at 11:30 when we saw your lights go on. We couldn't figure out what the problem was. We were concerned so we stayed up and watched past midnight. We can see everything from our roof."

"Yes," I said. "We heard footsteps on our roof so we called UN security."

"It was a cat," she said. "A big fat cat. He prowls the neighborhood at night. He used to walk on our roof. When I first heard it I was certain it was a human being. The sound was so humanlike. Nobody believed me. Then a bit later I saw the cat. Huge." She held her hands about a foot-and-a-half apart. "He catches birds and eats them right over there, next to your house."

I looked down and saw a pile of bird feathers.

"Well, I'd like to believe it was a cat," I said. "But I heard the sound and it was absolutely humanlike. I can't imagine a cat sounding like that."

"I couldn't either," she said. "But believe me, it was a cat. The roof material – it's made out of metal – makes his footsteps sound bigger. I know; it happened to me."

She said the cat was a nocturnal beast who rarely showed his face in the daytime. "Our neighbor down the street, he raises pigeons," she added, "and this big fat cat likes pigeons too. The neighbor has been hunting down that cat for months now, trying to protect his birds."

"Well, again, I hope you're right."

"Listen, Robert, I grew up in this neighborhood. It is a safe and quiet place, not like the rest of Tashkent, which is noisy like a whorehouse. I share your concern. It's in our interest that you're safe and happy. This is my neighborhood. We consider our neighbors to be part of our family. We want you to be safe."

"I'll tell Vlad what you have said. Meanwhile, if you ever see that fat cat, call me, okay, so I can take a look. And if we hear the noise again at night, can we call you so that you can look from your roof and try to identify the source of the sound?"

"Yes, any time."

We said goodby and I returned to our courtyard, where Vlad and Aziz were preparing to leave. I told them what Vasiliya had to say about the cat.

"That's ridiculous," Aziz said.

"If I were in her place I'd say the same thing," Vlad said. "It's in their interest to put things in the best light."

"Well, I hope she's right and that it was a big cat," I said.

"Dai Bog," Vlad responded. "Let God make it so."

Vlad and Aziz left, telling us to call them if we heard the sound again and to stay inside our house if we did. Vlad also wanted us to telephone if we ever saw someone in the house next door, which was supposed to be empty and whose roof provided the only conceivable, albeit very difficult, means of accessing our roof.

Later that day, when I returned home from an errand, our nanny told me she had heard footsteps on the roof while I was gone. And shortly thereafter a cat appeared in our courtyard, peering through the living-room window.

"Cat! Cat!" Ariel screamed.

Then, in the early evening, I saw a black and white cat on the roof of our neighbor's house. And this cat proceeded to jump onto the roof of our kitchen, where he remained, a short cat-jump from the second-floor roof of the main building. So it probably was a cat, after all, whom Eriko and I had heard the night before.

Further confirmation came in the evening. I was outside, on the street, chatting with another Uzbek couple who lived down the block.

"Have you ever heard about cats walking on the roofs of these houses?" I asked.

"Oh yes," one woman said. "All the time. At first I thought it was human. But it's a cat. We bang the ceiling with a broomstick and he scatters away."

LAW AND ORDER

15 November 2001 – A friend of mine – I'll call him "Ivan" – went to register his new car today. After spending eight hours waiting at the registration office, he finally spoke with the police official there. The officer made all kinds of unreasonable demands.

"You don't have a sticker on your rear bumper with blue and yellow stripes," the police official said.

"I need one?" Ivan asked.

"Yes. It's required."

"But if it's required why didn't the manufacturer put one there? The car, after all, was made here in Uzbekistan."

No response.

Then the official inspected a medical kit that Ivan kept inside in the car. "You don't have the proper analgesic," the officer said.

"But I *do* have an analgesic," Ivan replied; "one that won't adversely affect the heart."

"You don't have the proper analgesic," came the response.

Finally: "You need to come back here with the wife of the man who sold you the car. She needs to testify that the car was sold with her permission."

With that, Ivan pulled out his wallet and payed a bribe, the equivalent of four US dollars – a lot of money in a country where the average monthly wage is between twenty and thirty bucks. After the money was passed over, the registration was complete. And all of Ivan's problems withered away.

18 December 2001 – I've just returned from the US, where I was on a book tour. On the Uzbek Airways flight back home, I spoke with a flight attendant named Vladimir, a Russian who lives in Tashkent. He told me that he had had a bad year. "A few months ago I was questioned by the police in connection with the murder of some guy I know. I was in Paris working a flight at the time of the murder. The police called me in for questioning and I voluntarily went to see them. They held me for two days and placed me in an isolation cell. It was awful. I wasn't even in the country when the murder took place. In the end they demanded money and I had to pay two hundred dollars to get out."

28 December 2001 – Ivan was called in by the police yesterday for questioning in some criminal case in which a woman tax inspector had been murdered. The police claimed Ivan's cell-phone number had been found in the suspect's phone book. Ivan denied any knowledge of the event or of the suspect. He was released after being questioned for three hours. Afterwards, I asked Ivan if the police treated him with respect or were rough on him.

"It was unpleasant," Ivan said. "Six investigators spoke to me at separate times. They tried to exert psychological pressure. One said to me 'You did it' and walked out of the room. One would tell me I was free to leave, only to have another tell me I couldn't. They had me sitting in a place with other convicts. One guy said about himself, 'So I'll get five years; big deal.' That scared me. All of the investigators but one were Uzbek. One was Russian, like me, and he seemed to be trying to help me out. He told me the sooner I physically left the police station the better off I'd be. I told him I absolutely did not want to spend the night there, when none of the bosses was around, when they could try to beat something out of me. Eventually, after I wrote a statement about my whereabouts on the day of the crime, they let me go, telling me that I might be called again."

29 December 2001 – Ivan came to visit me this morning. He looked gaunt. He was unsmiling. His eyes were glazed over and teary. He looked awful, the worst I've ever seen him look.

"Come in," I said.

He proceeded to tell me what had transpired. "It has been awful. A nightmare. I was at the police station from 10:00 yesterday morning until 10:00 last night. They didn't let me eat. At the end of it I said, 'Look, I am distraught and I need to eat. Under no circumstances will I stay here overnight.' So they let me go and told me to come back at 11:00 A.M. today.

"They questioned me all day. It turns out the woman they said was a tax inspector may have been a prostitute. She was killed on 22 December. Somehow, among her effects, was a slip of paper with two telephone numbers on it. One of the numbers belonged to the phone in the apartment I own and rent. I have no idea how it got there. Perhaps it was written down improperly. The other number was for some organization, and on the back of the paper was the name of some Uzbek guy. But they questioned me about the apartment, about who has lived there. They called in my friend Dmitrii, who used to live there. They called in my mother. At one point yesterday I even had to go the station with my six-year-old son, because I had nobody else to take care of him. He faced the ordeal of watching his father being fingerprinted. It was very hard on him.

"One investigator shouted at me. 'You're guilty! We're going to put you in jail!' I was terrified. Another investigator lied to me. He said my name had been written on the slip of paper next to the apartment phone number. 'Impossible,' I said. I demanded to see the paper. Finally they showed it to me and my name wasn't there."

Ivan stopped talking and covered his face. He started to weep. After a few moments he regained his composure.

"I hate this country. I want to leave here."

Ivan left to return to the police station. He telephoned me a few hours later. His voice was lighter. '"I want to come by right now, okay?"

He arrived with a slight grin on his face. "It is finished," he said. "I am again a normal citizen of Uzbekistan. They let me go, and returned my passport to me. They did this after I started yelling at them. I told them I have been there three days already, and I had absolutely no connection to the murder. I told them I wanted to help and told them everything I knew. I said if this continued I would bring in friends from the procuracy, from the diplomatic corps, from the government. When the investigator saw I meant business, he backed off. 'No, no,' he said. 'That's not necessary. You are free to go.' I asked him, 'Can I tell everybody that there is nothing hanging over my head, that I am clean, that I am a normal citizen?' 'Yes, yes,' he said."

I took Ivan out for lunch to celebrate. "What kind of food would you like to eat?" I asked.

"It doesn't matter. Anything. I haven't been able to eat for three days."

We dined on Middle Eastern food at a restaurant called Omar Khayyam: tabouleh, hoummus, tomato and cucumber salad, steamed beef, basmati rice, green tea. But even during lunch, Ivan was tense.

"Be careful," he said to me in a soft voice. "Those two men sitting behind us look funny. They haven't stopped staring at our table. I think they might be from the security services."

We left the restaurant without incident. Ivan said he was looking forward to celebrating that evening by going bowling with his friends.

30 December 2001 – The police called Ivan back for questioning this morning. Two more hours' worth. Then they let him go, but told him to return at 4:00 P.M. He did so. And they asked him, "Do you have anything to say?"

Ivan said, "I have nothing to say to you."

"Get out of here. Leave," they said.

31 December 2001 – Ivan is distraught. "The police say I'm only a witness in the case, but they're treating me like a suspect. I am exhausted. I was out until midnight last night consulting with friends and with a lawyer. I decided to write a letter to the state prosecutor, and to the main prosecutor of the city, saying I am being harassed by the police and that I fear they will beat me up. I want to have this letter written now so that, if they do beat me, I can have something ready as proof of what they're doing. If they beat me, you know, I will confess to anything. There are some men who can endure this type of torture and not give in. I am not such a man. I have a weak heart. If they beat me I will say

what they want. If I don't come home one night then this letter can be used."

Ivan asks me whether the United Nations can grant him political asylum. "I don't want to live here any more. This is a country without laws. The police can do anything they want. There is no protection against them. Even if I get out of this situation okay, I don't want my son to grow up in this place. They could wind up doing the same thing to him. I am scared. And I don't know what to do."

Ivan never again heard from the police. The case, with respect to him, simply disappeared.

7 January 2002 – The police pulled over the car I was riding in today because, they said, I was wearing a seat belt. Nobody wears seat belts in Uzbekistan. The cops thought I had buckled up as a safety precaution because the driver had been drinking. Why else would someone buckle up?

4 March 2002 – A story from a taxi driver: "A cop stopped me and I got out of the car and he told me I was driving drunk. I said no way, absolutely not. Then I joked with him, telling him an anecdote about a cop who procured his baton at a sex shop. He laughed briefly and asked me for my documents. Then he told me again I was drunk. 'I am not,' I said. 'Let me smell your breath,' he said. I exhaled. 'You are drunk,' he said. 'Look,' I said, 'I am not. I do not drink.' He called over another cop. 'Breathe for him,' he said. I exhaled again. The second cop said, 'You're drunk. Come with us to the hospital.' At that point I said I would do so but only after I dropped off my passenger, who happened to be a big shot. 'Why are your driving him?' the first cop asked. 'He is my friend and I want to bring him to work,' I said. At that point, they let me

go. These people are scum. They treat you as if you are dirt. Had I not had my friend with me I would have wound up in some medical facility facing who knows what."

5 October 2002 – We were riding in a taxi today when a uniformed policeman stopped the vehicle. The driver exited the car. The officer told him, "I ran out of liquor. I need money to buy some vodka." The driver paid up, without even arguing. "I normally would have told the cop to go to hell," the driver later said. "But I admired his honesty. He didn't play games with me like they usually do."

8 May 2003 – I heard the following story today from Matt, an American friend of mine, concerning one of his Uzbek colleagues, whom I'll call "Farkhod." Not long ago, Farkhod was stopped by a cop, who asked him to open up the trunk of his car. Farkhod did so without concern, since this type of thing happens all the time. After a minute or so, the cop told Farkhod to go on his way, which he did. Then, a short distance down the road, Farkhod was stopped again, this time by several policemen. They opened up his truck and found some cocaine, which had been planted there by the first police officer. Matt said it cost Farkhod US$5,000 to make the problem go away.

5 June 2003 – A reliable source told me the following story today: "A couple of my friends were in a car accident yesterday. Not a big one. Just a little fender bender. Nikolai was behind the wheel. Sasha, who's Korean, was the passenger. A little Tika hit them from the rear. [Tika is a small car manufactured in Uzbekistan by Daewoo, a Korean company.] The two guys exited their car and approached the driver of the car that had hit them. 'What are you doing?' they

asked. The driver, a young woman of no more than twenty, started cursing them out. In particular she swore at Sasha, calling him a 'stinking Korean.' Sasha was incensed and slapped the girl on the ear. The girl's mother was in the car and bore witness. Later that day, the phone rang at Nikolai's house. His grandmother answered. The caller said he was from the electric company. He said there was an outstanding bill that Nikolai had to pay. The granny told the caller where Nikolai worked. Unfortunately, it wasn't the electric company calling. Turns out that the young female driver was a close relative of one of the heads of the Uzbek mafia. She or her mother must have taken down Nikolai's license plate number and, through their connections, obtained his phone number.

"The next day, two mafia bulldogs showed up at Nikolai's office. Sasha worked there as well. The thugs literally dragged Nikolai and Sasha away. Nobody could do anything about it. Colleagues tried to call the police, but the police didn't come. The bulldogs drove Nikolai and Sasha to a secluded location near the river. Then the mafia boss himself showed up. Nikolai said he had a big, big nose. The boss interrogated Nikolai and Sasha and determined that Sasha had slapped the girl. They sent Nikolai packing, but beat the shit out of Sasha. A police car drove by during all of this but didn't stop. There's Uzbek justice for you."

GODFATHERS AND CLANS

23 July 2004 – The United Nations Office on Drugs and Crime (UNODC) is one of the international community's leading crime-fighting organizations. Its mandate, as defined on its website – <unodc.org> – is "to assist Member States in their struggle against

illicit drugs, crime and terrorism." Headquartered in Vienna, UNODC has a network of twenty-one field offices worldwide, including a facility in Tashkent.

The UNODC has studied the nature of criminal organizations in Uzbekistan, based in significant part on a survey disseminated to the governments of Central Asia, including Uzbekistan.[54] I was given an unpublished UNODC report entitled "Transnational Organized Crime in Central Asia (1997–2003): A Survey and Assessment." It contains a rare, comprehensive look at the dark, powerful, criminal underbelly of Uzbekistan. It is the best source of information on the Uzbek mafia I have come across. For that reason, lengthy excerpts, below, are included in this book. A warning to readers and researchers: the writing is thick, and the reading is bumpy. But for those interested in Uzbekistan, the information is gold.

The countries of Central Asia emerged from the Soviet era with a significant criminal underworld and shadow economy, endemic corruption and a demoralized law enforcement and legal apparatus. This legacy provided a perfect context for the development of serious and sophisticated criminal organizations. Although none of the former Soviet republics has escaped a serious organized crime problem, the scale of the problem and its specific manifestations have varied from country to country. In Central Asia the organized crime problem initially revolved around drug trafficking, which is sometimes described in terms of the resurgence of the old Silk Road, albeit for illegal business, whereas in the Slavic states the illegal exportation of natural materials, extortion of business, and the hijacking of the privatization process loomed much larger. Yet to see organized crime in Central Asia only in drug trafficking terms is a mistake. Other criminal markets coexist with drug business and although some criminal organizations specialize in drug trafficking, others have a much broader portfolio. This includes trafficking in gold and precious metals. In Uzbekistan, "around 12 kg of pure gold have been confiscated from criminal elements, and criminal proceedings have been instituted against around 200 people for thefts of precious metals" ... Criminal organizations have also defrauded the state of natural resources, agricultural products and manufactured goods. Other sources of illegal proceeds include smuggling, tax evasion, tax fraud, as well as drugs and arms trafficking. In short, organized crime in Central Asia, like that in many other regions, is involved in a wide variety of criminal activities and markets. At the same time, organized crime in the region also has certain distinctive characteristics that need to be identified and elucidated.

Clan Based Organizations

One of the most significant features of organized crime groups in Central Asia and one that differentiates them from organized crime groups elsewhere in the post Soviet space is the importance of clan based relations. Because clan is such an important factor in social life, it is not surprising that many criminal groupings are based on tribal or clan connections. Clan affiliations along with notions of family and kinship and, to some degree, ethnic origin, act as bonding mechanisms and provide the trust that is an essential component of successful organized crime. Since many minorities also live in the particular localities or regions of one country, clan or kinship based organized crime in Central Asia sometimes has a geographical focus ...

The clan basis for organized crime, however, has significant implications that transcend geography or locality ... [C]lan affiliation has been an important linkage between government and organized crime at either the local or the national level. Where a leading member of a clan has a position of authority in local or central government or in law enforcement, this position is used to benefit other members of the clan through nepotism and other preferential decisions. If other members of the clan are involved in organized crime then they obtain a degree of protection that would otherwise have to be bought. As one commentary noted, corruption is not only about money or the use of public office for purely personal gain, "but rather it is part of a highly organized system of economic crime that permeates all aspects of life ... Clan networks and kinship links play an important role in orientating the police away from serving society equally and towards favoring their own. Many blame the corrupting link between relatives in the security forces and justice system on traditional kinship relationship within Uzbek, Kazakh and Kyrgyz and Tajik societies". From this perspective, it is highly probable that at least some of the crackdowns on organized crime by government and law enforcement agencies are carefully targeted against rival clans, while criminal organizations linked to the dominant clan obtain preferential impunity and are able to continue with the accumulation of criminal wealth. Although there might be a gradual trend away from groups based on a single ethnic identity or clan and towards more cosmopolitan criminal organizations, clan or family is likely to retain its importance as a major basis for organized crime for the foreseeable future.

Leadership

A second characteristic of organized crime in Central Asia is that each organization has strong leadership ... The leaders themselves usually exhibit one or more special qualities that elevate them above the rank and file of the criminal organization. While these characteristics vary *depending on the type of group and type of criminal activity, they generally include one or more of the following:*

- *Leading position or high status in a family or clan, which translates into a similar position in a family or clan-based criminal organization;*
- *Charisma, which is particularly important in ethnic or terrorist groups;*
- *A position of authority in government or public administration;*
- *Membership in the ruling party or dominant clan;*
- *Contacts with local or central authorities which can be used to facilitate criminal activities and provide a degree of immunity from law enforcement;*
- *A high position in law enforcement agencies, which can be translated into profits through bribery and extortion;*
- *Physical strength and the power of intimidation, qualities that are particularly important in "sportsmen" groups and small criminal gangs.*

Some of the leaders were bureaucrats or high-ranking officials in the Communist Party during the Soviet era or are currently members of the dominant political party. Their connections and relationships enable them to exert pressure on law enforcement or even on their government colleagues. They can also use their influence to obtain information about forthcoming law enforcement operations as well as about on-going investigations, thereby enabling their organizations to take effective counter-actions ...

Another quality that can sometimes contribute to leadership is previous business experience. The importance of this, however, depends largely on the types of crime that the group is engaged in.

It is particularly important, if not essential in the area of economic crimes such as embezzlement, fraud, misappropriation, and money laundering. It is far less important for criminal groups that confine their activities to common robberies or extortions. For major criminal organizations that are involved in both criminal activities and legitimate business this experience is particularly important.

Although little is known, at least in the public domain, about the actual leaders of organized crime in most Central Asian countries, the exception is Uzbekistan. Ironically, of the four Central Asian countries participating in the survey, only Uzbekistan failed to produce detailed responses to the questions concerning criminal organizations. This is somewhat ironic since although Uzbekistan has some small predatory organizations it also has a few large, organized criminal communities which have close links with members of the political elite. A clamp-down in the first few months of 1993, for example, uncovered more than 940 criminal organizations (including 10 armed militias), initiating more than 1,000 criminal proceedings, and returning 425 convictions including 22 for murder. Similarly, in 1995, for example, law enforcement detected and neutralized over 1,200 organized crime groups. For all these "successes", however, the larger and more powerful criminal organizations in Uzbekistan appear to have remained intact.

There are reportedly at least three major criminal organizations in Uzbekistan, as well as some Korean organizations with a strong base in the Ferghana Valley, a degree of control over trade with the Far East, and considerable influence in the restaurant business. The three major organizations all appear to have had strong leadership and strong political support.

One was reportedly led by Gafur Rakhimov, who had graduated from low level extortion in local markets and car theft to become perhaps the leading entrepreneur in the country, and, some would argue, the leading criminal.

A second criminal organization was led by Salim Abduvaliev (Salimov) who eventually bought the most prominent soccer team "Pakhtakor" along with the Central Stadium in Tashkent.

The third major criminal organization was Armenian based and ran the biggest market in Central Asia, the "Tashkent Racecourse". It was led by Gaborian until he was killed on December 31, 1995 by gunfire while taking some friends on a skiing outing.

Although there was some speculation that Gaborian's death was the result of a dispute with groups from the Caucasus, it came against a background of internecine criminal warfare, with the major groups trying to take over or eliminate their smaller rivals. Subsequently, Abdul Aziz, an Uzbek from Kazakhstan who supplied his friends with cars which were stolen in Germany and then "legally" imported into Uzbekistan was arrested. The other two major organizations, however, seemed to be able to act with a high level of impunity, and it was believed that they not only had strong connections with the political elite but also had patrons or protectors in the Cabinet. There have been allegations that both Rakhimov and Abduvaliev are closely linked to Timur Alimov, a key political figure and sporadically, at least, a close and influential adviser to President Karimov. Alimov's son reportedly worked for both criminal leaders and Alimov himself has been described as their "deputy" in the State machinery. At this point there is an important intersection and overlap between clan rivalry and organized crime. According to one analysis of clan competition in Uzbekistan, Alimov is a major representative of the Tashkent clan and the "Tashkent mafia"; his most important rival for Karimov's favor is Ismail Dzurabekov who reportedly enjoys the support of the "Samarqand mafia" and clan.

Although Alimov's relationship with Karimov – and consequently his political fortunes – has ebbed and flowed, the connection has been of great benefit to Rakhimov and Abduvaliev. With Alimov's help the two men gained control over key components of sports in Uzbekistan: "Salim Abduvaliev established control over football while Gafur Rakhimov was in control of boxing". In return for Alimov's patronage they offered to sponsor major sporting events in Uzbekistan, including the annual Tashkent tennis competition for the President's Cup. The relationship might well have gone a lot further than the provision of sporting events under the President's auspices. According to one report Rakhimov "is a personal adviser to the Uzbek President ... and performs his special, delicate tasks, including the relationships with the Russian leadership". Rakhimov has his own Moscow office and "enjoys unique influence in the Uzbek embassy, whose employees refer to him with fear. He has very strong influence in the economic and political leadership of Uzbekistan ... Without his unofficial sanction no single major economic project starts in Uzbekistan". He was also well connected both to the Yeltsin government and to Yuri Luzhkov, the Mayor of Moscow ...

Gafur Rakhimov is an intriguing figure and one who represents many of the paradoxes, contradictions, and ambiguities of the post-Soviet business world. Ostensibly one of Uzbekistan's leading entrepreneurs and certainly a philanthropist who has supported orphanages and children in need and created his own charitable foundation for this purpose, Rakhimov rose to international prominence in 2000 when, as an official with the Uzbek national boxing team, he was refused entry into Australia for the Sydney Olympic games. A member of the Executive Committee of the International Amateur Boxing Federation, Rakhimov, was reportedly of great interest to the FBI, the Russian MVD and French law enforcement *agencies, and on September 8, 2000, the Australian authorities declared that he was banned from entry into the country "for reasons of security". Although the International Olympic Committee was initially very unhappy at the decision, it was subsequently satisfied by the explanation provided by the Australian authorities.*

The Uzbek government, however, vigorously protested the ban. Rakhimov himself subsequently initiated defamation actions against the Australian Broadcasting Corporation (ABC) and British journalist Andrew Jennings, author of a book entitled The Great Olympic Swindle, *in which Rakhimov had been profiled, and against the* Sydney Morning Herald *and Jennings. He lost the case involving ABC but won the case against the* Sydney Morning Herald *and Jennings when the jury found that he had been portrayed as a "major international heroin dealer who killed, engaged in gun running, fraud and smuggling and had been defamed". Subsequently, in a New South Wales Supreme Court, Rakhimov won a libel action against Jennings who had claimed in his book that Rakhimov "had been engaged in fraud, prostitution, assassination, gun running and plutonium smuggling, that he was a gangster in the Soviet black economy and had traded sporting medals for bribes". In spite of this victory, however, Rakhimov remains a source of concern to several intelligence and law enforcement agencies outside Uzbekistan which believe that, at the very least, he has moved in the same circles as major criminal figures. Moreover, his status and prominence in Uzbekistan is not inconsistent with the notion of an organic relationship between leading criminal entrepreneurs and members of the political elite.*

The Australian refusal to allow him into the country was not the first such incident for Rakhimov. He has not been able to obtain a Schengen visa [a visa permitting entry to fifteen European Union countries] *and was denied entry into France when he landed at Le Bourget airport* on March 20, 1998. The French refusal seems to have been based on a memo emanating from France's Direction Generale de la Police Nationale, number 98-01093 (February 5, 1998) which portrayed Rakhimov as "one of the leading members of the Uzbek Mafia whose presence in France would constitute a grave threat to public security". In response to the publication of these details in the Intelligence Newsletter, a French publication, Rakhimov, also known as Ghafur Arslambek, claimed that no West European law and order departments or services had accused him of money laundering. He also sent the Intelligence Newsletter a series of documents from the Russian MVD and the head of the Interpol office in Tashkent confirming that he had no criminal record. In spite of these protestations of innocence, a British newspaper in 1998 had claimed that Rakhimov was well known to the British Criminal Intelligence Service and their Belgian counterparts as a major player in the drug business and even quoted a Belgian police source asserting that Rakhimov "should be the godfather of Tashkent".

Questions were also raised in the European Parliament about a potential business deal that Rakhimov was negotiating. The Danish beer company Carlsberg was considering renovating a brewery in Uzbekistan and using that as its outlet in Central Asia. Attempts were made to obtain funding for the project through the European Bank for Reconstruction and Development (EBRD). This prompted one of the Euro MPs to ask very publicly why the EBRD was cooperating with a citizen of Uzbekistan who took part in narcotics smuggling, associated with the mafia and was included on the Schengen "black list". The EBRD subsequently backed out of the project.

The dossiers on Rakhimov seem to be based in part on his presence at a party of organized crime figures in Prague on May 31, 1995. The party was held at the Black & White, a club owned by Semeon Mogilevich. It was broken up by Czech police who detained all those *who were there, photographed them and expelled them from the country. Rakhimov's presence at this meeting suggested that he was not simply a bit player in organized crime. Subsequently, the FBI concluded that Rakhimov had "a list of associates that put him in the premier league of the new eastern mafia". According to press reports, the FBI contended that Rakhimov "worked with (Russian organized crime figure Vyacheslav Kirilovich) Ivankov's lieutenants, the Kandov brothers, Mark and Boris, fronting one of their operations, a Vienna-based company called Agrotek".*

In addition to his alleged links with Ivankov, Rakhimov was reportedly connected to Sergei Mikhailov, one of the leaders of the Solntsevo criminal organization. This connection operated in part through business links. Rakhimov is the major owner of a Tashkent-based agribusiness group Agro Plus K and Mag, which is the most important company in the Uzbek cotton trade. Agro Plus K and Mag, however, also invested in Mikhailov's Russian company, SV Holding. There is also a Swiss company Agro Plus K&M which reportedly operates through a figurehead, Franz Kamenzind, who also manages yet another Agro Plus – trading in chemical and agricultural commodities – which operates from the same address. Swiss authorities reportedly believe that Rakhimov controls both these firms. There have also been allegations that Agro Plus K&M laundered dirty money from Russian organized crime and from members of the Uzbek Government. Agro Plus K&M reportedly signed a long-term contract with the Austrian firm Agrotek, which is controlled by Rakhimov but believed to be part of Ivankov's business conglomerate. Sums up to 20 million dollars were recorded moving into and through the accounts of Agro plus K&M at different times. The picture is muddied further by the fact that Agro Plus K&M in Tashkent is sometimes represented by another company, Vita, which is a Belgian–Uzbek joint venture; significantly, Rakhimov *is registered as the President of yet another company in Belgium – G & K International, a management consultancy firm. Another affiliate of Agro Plus in West Europe is the Eurofood International company founded in Paris in 1996. Starting with a minimum registered capital of 50,000 French francs ($8,190), the company posted sales of 15 million French francs in 1996, and revenue of 265 million French francs in 1997. In April 1998 the registered capital was increased to one million French francs but then in May 1999, Eurofood International was suddenly wound up. Significantly, the "majority shareholder in Eurofood was the Norel Holding BV company, represented by Artur Martirosian, a Russian-Israeli businessman nicknamed the 'Armenian' who is also managing director of Agro Plus in Tashkent".*

Although Rakhimov strongly denies his involvement in any wrong-doing, his known associations combined with what appears to be a deliberate lack of transparency in his business dealings suggest that at least some of the allegations against him are well-founded. Moreover ... the Kazak authorities in their response to the United Nations questionnaire on transnational organized crime mentioned that both Rakhimov and Abduvaliev were attempting to take over some criminal operations in Kazakhstan. The main point to emphasize here though is that organized crime in Uzbekistan has strong leaders, who operate both in the licit and illicit sectors and who bring to their businesses of all kinds a high degree of entrepreneurial skill and flair as well as considerable political influence.

30 June 2004 – Among expats in Uzbekistan, Charles Rudd is the Godfather, in the best sense of the word. The American entrepreneur has been working in and around the former Soviet Union for nearly three decades, always on the lookout for business opportunities. Rudd, who has lived in Uzbekistan since 1988, is President

and Founder of InterConcepts, Incorporated. According to Rudd, the company provides "consulting and engineering services, enterprise restructuring and privatization, project management, representation, joint venture creation and supervision of investments, product registration and distribution, property management, and market research." InterConcepts works in the following business sectors in Uzbekistan: construction materials and technology, satellite navigation and internet services, military and civil telecommunications, agricultural technology, computer systems, graphic arts and publishing, and pharmaceuticals.

In short, Charles Rudd has seen a lot. And he knows a lot. His seventeen years in Uzbekistan makes him one of the most senior and experienced foreign observers around. I met with him at his Tashkent office with the intention of talking about the Uzbek economy. In the three-and-a-half years I had lived in Uzbekistan, the government had enacted a series of stringent measures designed, ostensibly, to protect Uzbek commerce from shoddy foreign goods and to promote the growth of domestic production. The measures, whatever their purpose, had put a lot of people out of work, especially small-time merchants and importers, and had deprived normal people of access to much needed consumer goods. The government's actions were the talk of the town:

- In May 2002, a fifty per cent customs tax was imposed on imported food items, and a ninety per cent duty was placed on nonfood items (the level was subsequently reduced to seventy per cent).[55] Taxes in the retail and food service system were also increased.[56]
- In January 2003, the border with neighboring Kazakhstan was sealed, shutting off a marketplace that many thousands of

Uzbeks regularly visited. It was an effort, the government said, to quell the spread of food poisoning from foreign foodstuffs.[57]

- In November 2004, Uzbek traders, historically a free-wheeling bunch, were required to obtain a new government license to sell their wares, and they were barred from acquiring foreign goods the way they usually did – via intermediary wholesalers.[58]

President Karimov explained the measures this way: "If we continue to fill our domestic market with low-quality imported goods, we put ourselves onto the list of undeveloped countries that, despite being rich with raw materials and more importantly, with a qualified labor force, can't build an appropriate economy, and can't produce its own quality consumer goods."[59]

Traders in Uzbekistan had previously engaged in the brisk import of foreign items, which were widely available on the shelves of the nation's bazaars and food stores. Russian yogurts and candies, European razors, imported music CDs, children's toys from China – these were just a few of the items I regularly used to see. After the government's decrees, these items mostly vanished, because wary entrepreneurs were no longer able to import them, or were unwilling to risk confrontations with the tax police over their ongoing under-the-table transactions.

Uzbekistan is a country of traders. Historically, it was a key link in the Silk Road. So merchants reacted to the measures negatively, often vehemently so. Rare public protests occurred.

In July 2002, merchants went on strike for several days in some of Tashkent's bazaars, including Chorsu, the city's largest. A friend of mine reported seeing shopkeepers throwing vegetables at tax police in Yunusubad, another of Tashkent's open-air markets.

In November of that year, Chorsu and other bazaars across the country again shut down.[60]

In November 2004, disturbances took place in the city of Kokand, where a crowd reported to number at least six thousand burned police cars and roughed up some tax inspectors. Protests also took place in the town of Margilan, in Ferghana City, and in Kashkadarya province. Several independent journalists in Uzbekistan described these events as "the most serious expression of popular discontent in recent memory."[61]

At the end of 2004, on 15 December, the US Embassy in Tashkent issued the following warning:

> The US Embassy in Uzbekistan urges the American community in Uzbekistan to exercise increased vigilance when shopping at area bazaars, especially Chorsu bazaar. Over the past week, Chorsu bazaar has experienced increased tensions between police and the local community. Please quickly exit the area if you witness any confrontation at one of the bazaars.

I asked Charles Rudd what was going on. I expected his answer to focus on macroeconomic theory Uzbek style. Instead, he spoke mostly about the clans. You can't talk about Uzbekistan's economy, Rudd said, without talking about the clans. Here is some of our conversation:

"If you look deep into history you'll find that Uzbekistan's economy evolved around tribal and clan structures," he said. "There was never a free economy. It was special interest. You had certain interests controlling cotton, another controlling trade."

And those interests, he said, were the clans.

"We define the so-called clan structure as having several manifestations. It could be an extended family, where the players are actually related; or you could see them as more of a criminal clan, the Gafurs and Salims.

"But at the same time you had clan structures which would be [region based]: the Tashkent clan, or Samarkand clan and Ferghana clan or the clan in Bukhara. And those tended to evolve out of two evolutionary roots. One was the way the country was divided up before the Soviet takeover – into emirs and whatever. If you look at this historical pattern, this was in a sense a tribal clan division. And you saw that they evolved in centers where people could defend their interests: people in Samarkand or Tashkent controlling trade routes, or someone in Ferghana or Kokand defending areas of agriculture. Even today the economy is very closely related to that. So, for example, if you want to get into mobile telephones, you'd deal with what we would call the PEP's, the 'politically exposed persons' who in effect control that sphere of business."

I asked Rudd to be specific. He pointed to the Karimov family.

"In terms of the current era," he said, "we could look at the presidential family and in particular the oldest daughter [Gulnora Karimova] who has been very active in purchasing and getting control over relatively strategic elements of industry, for example, in cement. And you've got Uzdonrobita [a large cell-phone enterprise] that has been purchased and under her control. And a great deal of the prestigious restaurants are now under her control."[62]

Everybody in Tashkent understood the reach of Gulnora Karimova's power. On the street, she and her sister Lola were viewed as crown princesses, able to leap tall buildings in a single bound, able to acquire lucrative businesses with a single gulp. The swanky fitness club on Pushkin Street? Yes, owned by one of the daughters. The fancy restaurant named Diyor? Gulnora just

up. The joke around town was that if a business enter-
me too successful, one of the crown princesses would
take it over. Better to fall on your face, business-wise.

All this fostered resentment among the normal folk of
Uzbekistan. My neighbor, for instance, an Uzbek worker of modest means, and by no means a political animal, once told me, out of
the blue, "We used to have money here. We used to have work. Not
any more. Karimov is too greedy. All he thinks about is himself and
his two daughters."

The Karimov clan, as Charles Rudd explained, is just one of
many family and regionally based organizations that wield power in
Uzbekistan. Clan impact on the economy, and on politics, was the
subject of a remarkable report released by the International Crisis
Group (ICG), a private think-tank. Entitled "Uzbekistan's Reform
Program: Illusion or Reality" and published on 18 February 2003,
the report lays out the breadth of clan activity in Uzbekistan, and the
overlap between clan leaders, economics, and politics. The report
states that "clans have become interlaced with the government"[63]

> Key ministers are grouped in competing blocs based both on clan
> or regional affiliation and on personal financial interests. The
> basis of these groupings is sometimes described in terms of
> regional clans: the Tashkent, Samarkand and Ferghana clans
> being the most influential. It is true that there has been a regional
> basis to some political–business groupings but this is not the only
> factor in how individuals cooperate: much revolves around
> access to financial resources, and such groupings are more flex-
> ible than a strict regional clan basis would suggest.
>
> Nonetheless, at its most simplistic, the political battle can be
> explained in terms of struggles between these groupings, and pri-
> marily between a Samarkand grouping, led by Ismail Jurabekov,

presidential adviser on agriculture and water resources, and Timur Alimov, viewed as head of a Tashkent clan, and an official in the presidential administration. This analysis places senior figures in one or the other camps, with the powerful interior minister Zohirjon Almatov, for example, being linked to Jurabekov, while SNB [state security] chief Rustam Inoyatov is linked to the opposing Alimov camp.

In reality, the situation is more complex, with several centers of power, and alliances among groupings shifting on issues and personalities. An appreciation of these key players and their allies is important to understanding why the process of reform is so difficult.

Much of retail trade and import/export operations is largely under the control of Deputy Prime Minister Mirabror Usmanov, who among other interests, controls the Ardus chain of supermarkets. [Ardus has a major presence in Tashkent.] First Deputy Prime Minister Kozim Tulyaganov, a former mayor of Tashkent, is alleged to have widespread property interests. Elior Ganiev, promoted to Deputy Prime Minister in November 2002, has considerable influence in foreign trade issues, and is closely linked to the security forces, which form an increasingly powerful political bloc. Indeed, interior minister Zohirjon Almatov is probably the most powerful successor to Karimov. SNB chief Rustam Inoyatov, linked to the Tashkent clan, is considered a rival of the interior minister and has a potent combination of intelligence on all members of the elite and considerable financial resources through family businesses ...

In all cases, government ministers have been deeply involved in a system of corruption in which they have achieved significant personal wealth. Any serious structural reform will undermine their chief sources of income, which tend to come from control over commodity exports or licensing of business activities, in other words from government control over the economy.

Lessening that control – introducing market reforms – would immediately reduce their economic power, and their political and social control.[64]

I wondered how a foreign businessman like Charles Rudd could operate in Uzbekistan. "The economy is run very much on the self-interest of a handful of players involved," I said. "Do you accept bribery and corruption as part of doing business? How do you maneuver between these clans and business groups, which are all interlaced with the government?"

"You have to look at the economy as a plane that is populated by large animals," Rudd said. "Like rhinoceroses and elephants and huge meat-eating dinosaurs. And we are the field mice and little, fast-moving, inconspicuous animals who have to move quicker and faster and stay out of the way of these large animals. You don't build houses or dens that are visible that can be trampled or taken over. So you keep moving, you keep extremely low. You know that if you're trapped in some corner you'll be destroyed. You have to take that as part of the risk to doing business here. But none of us accepts the fact of all of the bribery and the dirty aspects of it because we're not going to get dirty like the other players. So if you have any business principles, you know that is going to limit where you are going to enter in terms of a field of business. If I see a business that's dominated by any one of these particular clan groups, the only way that I could ever enter that business is to be some kind of a participant of a minor contractor sitting under the roof of that particular clan, in a sense protected by that large animal or dinosaur from other competing ones who would come and enter.

"I can't speak for other people here, but we have changed our business profile from the days when I could openly provide lots of high-tech equipment in the medical field or lasers or computers and telecommunication. We have downsized and we're a very, very small company that provides mainly services. So I don't get involved in any retail or commercial trade that would be perceived to be competitive to any of these particular [clan] interests."

THE BEST EDUCATION MONEY CAN BUY

26 July 2004 – Matthew Walkley, a British educator, is Dean of Students at Westminster International University in Tashkent, one of Uzbekistan's most prestigious institutions of higher learning. The university is a joint venture between Uzbekistan and Great Britain. Curriculum and performance standards are set by the University of Westminster, which is based in London. The students are all Uzbek citizens – the nation's best, brightest, and – given the university's pricey tuition – among the wealthiest. Walkley took up his post in 2002. He told me today he has just resigned, disheartened by much of what he has experienced.

Walkley had an insider's view of Uzbek education and spoke to me candidly about one of Uzbekistan's quaint little habits: bribery. My Uzbek friends had often spoken of corruption in the schools: of the need to pay "gifts" to get their kids into this or that college or institute or, in the case of one friend, to get his son into a well-regarded grammar school. Walkley's experiences confirmed that school-based corruption is rampant.

There was an Uzbek professor at Westminster, Walkley said, who had been working on the side tutoring prospective students. Walkley wanted the professor fired, because his activities created the impression that the applicants were buying their way into the university, thereby circumventing the normal, competitive application process. "So there was a disciplinary hearing with the Rector and I went through a long list of things that weren't satisfactory about this professor's performance," Walkley said. "And then I began to lose confidence, and I said maybe we should give him a second chance, a chance to improve. Then one of my colleagues, who was the Registrar of the university at that time, a close colleague, a close friend, a very straight guy, he said, 'Well, before you go on, let me tell you something else. Yesterday the professor came to me and he offered to buy an advance copy of the entrance test so he could share it with his tutees, and he offered to share the proceeds [derived from releasing the test] with the Registrar.' So after that I said, it's clear, we've got to sack him. I don't know what kind of money was offered. But I've heard from other people that upon entrance to a university quite large sums change hands, thousands of dollars. I've heard four thousand quoted for entrance to places like Tashkent State Technical University and Tashkent State Law Institute. So they're not small amounts of money by local standards."

"Typically," Walkley explained, "if you're trying to bribe your way into a university, the money goes to the Dean and above. Another member of our staff, who's not working on the lecturing side, has previously worked as a lecturer at another university. She's a Russian woman. Very intelligent. Very well read. A well-rounded individual. Very interesting to speak to. She was talking to me one day about the bribery system, particularly in relation to assessments.

"Working in a local university, she had some students in her class who never turned up. In the local system, attendance is assessed. If you don't attend all the time, you can be expelled from the university, so attendance is monitored quite closely."

Walkley said his colleague observed three kinds of bribery: (1) students who skipped class would pay off the Dean. "And then (2) you get students in class who, you know, if they're struggling, they may pay the lecturer. Then (3) you get lecturers who make it impossible for students to pass. Students know they have to come and offer some inducement to get through. And she said that wherever the money comes in, some of it gets passed up the hierarchy, so deans pass it on to deputy rectors, and on upwards, and even rectors are passing it on to the local mayor or people in local government."

Walkley said his colleague never took bribes. "She said she didn't need to or want to take bribes. She said it was quite lonely because she was in the minority, and perhaps treated with a bit of suspicion by those who were in the bribery system. She said she went in and did her work and went home. But she was – ostracized would be putting it a bit too strongly – but she felt on the outside as one of the lecturers who weren't involved in this. Which again suggests that taking bribes is the norm rather than the exception."

Walkley said even Westminster students have been known to offer bribes.

"Salaries in our university are not that high," he said. "And low salaries are an incentive to take bribes, just in order to survive. I was appraising staff last week and one of the law lecturers told me twice this semester he had been approached by students to give a higher mark. They were offering a hundred dollars. He's earning currently a hundred dollars a month. And the approach came from the students' parents to his parents. The parents of the students phoned the teacher's parents to ask if there was anything to be done and offered this sum of money. They were all Uzbeks. He said he refused. Who knows whether he took any of that money, or whether any of the other staff are receiving similar offers. Some of them must be falling to temptation. One hundred dollars a month in Tashkent compares reasonably well with what lecturers are officially earning in other [Uzbek] universities, but not well with what they earn after taking bribes. It's certainly not enough to live comfortably in Tashkent. So people must be taking money."

Walkley said Westminster International University's Registrar is a special target of bribe givers. "She's a young woman, and at this time of year [summertime] parents are coming by knocking on her door all the time to ask about the entrance procedures. And she's constantly turning away gifts.

"I went in the office the other day and there was a nice little oil painting on the seat. A parent had brought this by as a sort of thank you for advice. And she had refused it. They refused to take it away and she just left it on the seat where they put it. A few days later the Rector came along and took the picture to give back to the parents. The Registrar also had also been offered a holiday in Turkey. So parents do come by. They don't always offer a direct bribe. They use a certain language: 'Is there anything we can do to help? Is there anything we can do to help our son get into the university?'"

Walkley said bribery in the schools has long been "a widespread practice. Absolutely ... Talk to anyone who has been through the local education system. I have a course leader [let us call her "Lena"], and she's the straightest person you could ever hope to meet, sort of a God-fearing Christian, very conscientious, very, very decent. She'll tell me even she has paid bribes in her undergraduate education. She came up against one or two lecturers where there was simply no alternative, because they're going to fail you, however well you perform. They're going to set the standard to a point where you'll fail. So you have to come and make an arrangement with them. It cuts both ways. Sometimes it's the lecturer pressing on the students for a bribe rather than the students initiating and going in and paying. Sometimes the class will get together collectively and nominate someone to go in and hand over a sum of cash to get around a difficult lecturer."

As for Westminster International, Walkley said, with pride, that ten per cent of his students fail each year. They are not allowed to move on. "We're still assessing with a certain amount of integrity," he said. "The system hasn't totally collapsed."

WORLD PRESS FREEDOM DAY

3 May 2004 – Today is World Press Freedom Day. Here is what the US Department of State said about freedom of the press in Uzbekistan in 2003:

> The Government employed official and unofficial means to restrict severely freedom of speech and the press, and an atmosphere of repression stifled public criticism of the Government. Although the law prohibits formal censorship, the Government warned editors that they were responsible for the content of their publications, and new amendments to the media law encouraged self-censorship. Ordinary citizens remained circumspect in criticizing the Government publicly.[65]

To commemorate World Press Freedom Day, a number of international organizations held a forum at the Intercontinental Hotel in Tashkent. Uzbek journalists attended, as did at least one representative of the Uzbek government. I was not there, but Reinhardt Krumm was. Krumm is head of the Tashkent office of the Friedrich Ebert Foundation, a German nongovernmental organization and one of the event's sponsors. Here are his notes regarding what happened when one plain-speaking Uzbek journalist stood up and spoke to the audience:

> "We should face reality," the journalist said. "We have a dictatorship in Uzbekistan. If the dictator says 'we should do this' then we should exactly do it, and if he says we shouldn't do it, then we shouldn't do it. You call that freedom of the press? Look at our two biggest papers: *Pravda Vostoka* and *Narodnoe Slovo*. The quality is so bad, that even fish would be disgusted to be wrapped in them.
>
> "All of a sudden the government is complaining about Western influence, but at the same time the government is involved in 'bizness' and 'entrepreneurship.' But if it comes to political values like human rights or freedom of press, they don't want to know anything about it."
>
> Later, the head of the Committee for Press (a government guy) stood up in the audience, shaking with fury:
>
> "You should be thankful that this event takes place." (laughter from the audience). "Why do you laugh? Why do you smear Uzbekistan? Don't you know that we have so many newspapers, so many journals that can be printed freely?" (more laughter). "Don't you know that there are websites that you can access without any problem? Why do you only criticize and not see the progress that we are making?"
>
> (Then his mobile phone rang and he answered it right in the microphone, causing further laughter in the audience.)
>
> A woman said, "Can I say something?" He said "No." She said "Yes." He said, yelled "NO!" and added, "I know your kind. You write badly so you're fired and then you get money from international organizations so you can write for them. I know your kind."

I was curious to know what happened to the journalist who spoke out at the meeting. I asked Allison Gill, chief researcher at Human Rights Watch in Tashkent, if she could find out. A few weeks later, Gill emailed me: "An independent journalist who runs a website called Ozod Ovoz (Free Voice) had his website shut down after he made a statement on 3 May, Press Freedom Day, that there is no freedom of speech in Uzbekistan; a local official from the press department got very angry and threatened the journalist to retaliate. The journalist thinks this is why his site was shut down."

CIVILITY AND HUMAN RIGHTS

17 February 2005 – I'm back in New York now, and some friends from Uzbekistan visited us this week. The husband, an ethnic Uzbek, is in his late thirties. The wife, also Uzbek, is in her late twenties. They have a small son, nearly three years old. One day the son got upset at his parents. The little boy started to swear up a mean streak, cursing out both Mama and Papa. I found his behavior disrespectful and shocking. The mother, however, looked up and smiled. "Oh, it's no big deal," she said. "He's an Uzbek boy."

Out of the mouths of babes comes the lexicon they hear at home. Papa doubtless dabbles in profane speech in front of the boy, and Mama not only puts up with it but shrugs it off as normal behavior.

I never found Uzbekistan to be a particularly gentle place. Civility, to be sure, doubtless exists in large doses among the many decent people of that country. My wife and I counted dozens of such people as our friends, including the family with the foul-mouthed toddler. But these friends would be the first to acknowledge – as

Mama's words indicate – that there is a rough edge in Uzbek culture, in the way the men treat the women, in the way bosses treat employees, in the way the haves treat the have-nots, in the way the powerful treat the powerless.

One Uzbek female friend, a member of the intelligentsia – I'll call her "Nodira" – explained it in terms of gender. Uzbekistan, she said, is a place where men mean more than women. "Our men are traditionalists," she observed. "They were raised in a patriarchal world in which the man is the head of the family. He decides everything; he has the final word. That's not to say that women can't influence things. But the man has the final say."

A recent survey of Uzbek women, conducted by the Uzbek Ministry of Health and the Uzbek State Department of Statistics, provides some revealing, relevant data. Married women were asked whether they had a say in deciding certain family issues. The survey reported,

The only specified decisions in which a majority of married women say they participate (either decide alone or make the decision with another person) is using contraception (72 per cent) and what food to cook each day (62 per cent). Only 43 per cent of married women participate in decisionmaking about their own health care, and only one in four has the final say. Almost half of married women (45 per cent) report that their husbands alone have the final say in their own health care. About 4 in 10 married women participate in decisionmaking about visits to friends and whether or not to work for money. Approximately one-third make decisions about daily household purchases and visits to family or relatives, but only about one-fifth report that they are involved in decisions regarding large household purchases. When married women are not involved in household decisionmaking, the data show that husbands are the ones most likely to be making the relevant decision alone.[66]

The survey also inquired about wife beating, a widespread problem in Uzbekistan. Wives were asked "whether a husband is justified in beating his wife under a series of circumstances. Possible circumstances that justify a man beating his wife included burning the food, arguing with him, going out without telling him, neglecting the children, and refusing sexual relations." The survey said that "seventy per cent of women agree with at least one of the specified reasons justifying a husband beating his wife. Women are most likely to agree for the following reasons: if she goes out without telling him (sixty-one per cent), if she neglects the children (fifty-nine per cent), or if she argues with her husband (forty-eight per cent). Women are less likely to agree that beating is justified if the wife burns the food or refuses to have sex with her husband (twenty-eight and twenty-one per cent, respectively)."[67]

This was a survey conducted by the Uzbek authorities. Seventy per cent of wives questioned said there are circumstances that justify wife beating. Twenty-eight per cent agreed that if they burn the food it is okay for their husbands to hit them. As I've said, Uzbekistan is not a very gentle place.

Ideally – at least according to my ideals – marriages are equal partnerships. In Uzbekistan they are not. The men are superior in the home, and they were raised to be that way. If a man is conditioned at home to act in a superior manner, sheer logic suggests that men will flaunt domestically inspired arrogance outside the home as well: in the workplace, on the streets, any place where the man believes he has the power and his associates or underlings do not.

Matthew Walkley, the former Westminster International University Dean, tells the following story about male arrogance at the highest level, as practiced by a man named Rustam Azimov, and witnessed by Walkley.

It was in May 2003, Walkley said, when the university's newly renovated building was officially to open. President Karimov himself was to pay a visit to give his blessings. The local Uzbek management, Walkley said, and the Rector in particular, were anxious, desperate to ensure that the place looked good for the Uzbek leader. "There was a feeling of panic really, and fear, fear of just making a mistake."

In the days before Karimov's visit, management cracked down. They forced students (who were preparing for exams) and teachers (who had already worked full days) to stay at the university well past midnight, rehearsing various scenarios designed to please Karimov. It was evidence, said Walkley, of a "casual lack of respect for the individual, which comes out a bit more strongly at times of pressure."

Walkley said the Uzbek government official in charge of the university was Rustam Azimov, the Minister of Economics. Azimov is one of the most powerful government officials, also holding the portfolio of First Deputy Prime Minister.

"He's a small, bullying kind of individual," Walkley observed. "He's actually, by the standards of the Uzbek government, a liberal. But by the standards of Western managment he's pretty much a dictator."

Walkley said Azimov took personal control of preparation for Karimov's visit. "He would come around the building and shout at the Rector and sort of humiliate him in front of his subordinates. And the Rector was getting more and more cowed over this period of time. On the day of the opening he looked really, really sick with worry and fear. I mean his whole body language – his shoulders were rounded, his head was down, and he looked really, really fearful. Things turned out fine, but it was interesting to see the change in his persona over that period. And at the same time that he looked almost broken, he became much more aggressive and bullying towards his inferiors, and this is a reflection, I suppose, of the system, in that each level bullies the level below. And that's the way they maintain control."

Walkley recalled how Azimov behaved when he interacted with students. "He would walk into a class and see these students, and he'd say, 'Oh, these students, their hair is too long.' And at eleven o'clock at fucking night he'd call for a barber to have their hair cut."

Walkley said Azimov also complained to the Rector about one male student who wore an earring and dressed in an off-beat manner. "Azimov said this student should be expelled. And he was serious. He was not joking. We didn't expel him and the student stayed, but it says something about the mentality."

A mentality rooted in arrogance. Behavior that is disrepectful. A sense, as Matthew Walkley put it, that "each level bullies the level below." The bullying most often felt by the average Uzbek is dealt by the police. Here is what the US State Department's 2003 Country Report on Human Rights Practices in Uzbekistan said: "Police routinely and arbitrarily detained and beat citizens to extort bribes."[68]

Some sense of how normal Uzbeks react to all this came in late March and early April 2004, when a series of suicide bombings and gunbattles broke out in Tashkent. A house used for making bombs also blew up in Bukhara. At least forty-three people were killed, most of them terrorists. The violence spread over four days and appeared primarily to target the police. A suicide bomber attacked a police gathering point in Tashkent's Chorsu market, killing three policemen. Three other officers were killed in two separate assaults, and an explosion took place near a police checkpoint.[69]

The Uzbek government blamed Islamic extremists, allegedly linked to al Qaeda. On the streets of Tashkent, however, there was little sympathy for the government. One man, a taxi driver, told me, "It is hard to tell who the real terrorists are – the ones with the bombs, or the ones in green police uniforms." The terrorists, he said, "don't want to hurt us. They want to hurt the people who have tormented us for so long with their police stops, their bribe-taking, their disrespect."

Another man, a wealthy Uzbek entrepreneur, said the terrorist attacks were "all Karimov's fault." "People are sick of him," the man said. "He has been in office too long. He has allowed the system to fall apart. He has allowed all the corruption. He has allowed poverty to spread all over the country. So what happened isn't all that unexpected."

A third man, a religious Muslim, said, "We Muslims pray for good health, for peace. And me, I pray for Karimov to die."

On 30 July 2004, another round of suicide bombings shook Tashkent. The General Prosecutor's office was hit. So were the perimeters of the US and Israeli embassies. At least two people died. The bombers – Islamic extremists again were said to be the likely perpetrators – seemed to be sending a mixed message: the Karimov regime, and especially its law and order apparatus, were bad; and so were the Americans and the Israelis, who cooperate with Karimov.[70] The July suicide attacks also coincided with the trial of fifteen people linked to the violence in March.

There are several aspects to consider with regard to these acts of terror.

From the perspective of the Uzbek government, and of Karimov in particular, the violence is the continuation of an effort by Islamic extremists to destabilize Uzbekistan with the ultimate aim of ousting the Uzbek President and establishing an Islamic state. It is an effort that dates back to the 1990s and, before 2004, reached an apex in February 1999, when car bombs hit the Uzbek Cabinet of Ministers building and other government targets in Tashkent, killing at least sixteen. This, doubtless, is an opinion shared by many Uzbek citizens.

There are many others in Uzbekistan, as I found in Tashkent, who reacted to the violence with equanimity, with a sense of "What else do you expect will happen to a regime where the few rule the many, where poverty is widespread, where the police are seen as bullies?"

And then there is the overarching issue of human rights. Narrowly focused, that issue, with regard to the terrorist acts, focuses on the police follow-up, on whether innocent people were swept up in the wave of arrests that followed each spate of violence; and whether suspects can get a fair trial. More broadly speaking, the question is whether, at some point down the road, terrorists – or some less drastic form of political opposition – may strike a chord among a population that feels its government has let them down, let them down by failing to improve their economic well-being, by depriving them of the basic sustenance of human rights, like freedoms of speech and religion.

Much has been written about human rights in Uzbekistan. I will not repeat in detail here what already is widely known: that Uzbekistan's human rights record is poor; that its government and its leader are authoritarian; that there is no genuine representative democracy; that criticism of the President is not only not tolerated but against the law;[71] that freedom of religion, and of Islam in particular, is restricted to those who practice their religion the way the state sees fit; that the police and organs of state security engage in the use of torture; that the judiciary is not independent. For anyone wishing to learn more, go to the US Department of State's annual human rights reports (<www.state.gov>) or to the work of Human Rights Watch (<www.hrw.org>), in particular their report *Creating Enemies of the State: Religious Persecution in Uzbekistan* (2004).

What I would like to convey is the gist of a conversation I had about human rights – and then some – with Craig Murray, who served as the United Kingdom's ambassador to Uzbekistan from 2002 to 2004. It was, to my mind, the single most interesting discussion I had over the course of my stay in Uzbekistan.

THE BRITISH AMBASSADOR

20 July 2004 – The first time I saw Craig Murray he was wearing a kilt. It was at a reception commemorating Romania's independence day. Many foreign ambassadors were there, as were many Uzbek government officials. They all wore suits and ties. The British Ambassador, adorned in knee-length tartan, stood out.

I had heard of Craig Murray several weeks before. He had made a speech, on 17 October 2002, and that speech had made news. (Ambassadors' speeches generally do not make news.) With a candor unusual for diplomats, Murray had ripped into Uzbekistan's human-rights performance.

"Uzbekistan is not a functioning democracy, nor does it appear to be moving in the direction of democracy," he said. "The major political parties are banned; parliament is not subject to democratic election, and checks and balances on the authority of the executive are lacking. There is worse: we believe there to be between seven and ten thousand people in detention whom we would consider as political and/or religious prisoners. In many cases they have been falsely convicted of crimes with which there appears to be no credible evidence they had any connection."

Murray went on to cite the treatment of two prisoners who had been "apparently tortured to death by boiling water." "But all of us know that this is not an isolated incident. Brutality is inherent in a system where convictions habitually rely on signed confessions rather than on forensic or material evidence. In the Uzbek criminal justice system the conviction rate is almost 100%. It is difficult not to conclude that once accused by the Prokurator there is no effective possibility of fair trial in the sense we understand it."

The Uzbek government does not particularly like Craig Murray. In May 2004, neither did I. Murray lived a few blocks away from my house, in an Uzbek mahalla, or residential neighborhood. On two evenings, one week apart, late at night, fireworks had been set off from Murray's backyard. They were intended to celebrate expansion of the European Union and the Queen's birthday. I was upset, and tracked down the ambassador's email address. I sent him the following note:

Dear Mr. Ambassador,

I live in the same mahalla you do, a few blocks from your home. It is, as you know, entirely a residential area.

I am all for EU expansion. And I respect the Queen as much as the next American. But Mr. Ambassador, I have two small children who go to bed at 9pm. Last night, your fireworks event – at 10:45pm – woke up my 22 month old daughter, who is ill with a fever. It took me a half hour to calm her down and get her to go back to sleep. A few weeks ago, your fireworks, which took place after 9pm, scared the shit out of my sleeping son, who is 5, and also disturbed my daughter.

And on both occasions the explosions woke up every damn dog within a 2 kilometer radius. Arf. Arf.

In the future, I'd be most grateful if you could refrain from late evening pyrotechnic expressions of celebration, inasmuch as you do, after all, live in a residential area. In the colonies, where I come from, we have zoning restrictions against this kind of thing.

With respect,
Robert Rand

P.S. Fireworks aside, I do admire you very much for the candor with which you have spoken out regarding the local government and its various policies.

A few days later, Murray sent me this reply:

Robert

Many thanks for your email. I am really very sorry if we awoke/scared your children.

I think we have a cultural difference here. In the UK it is very much part of popular culture to let off fireworks from your own back garden, even when it is a very small garden in a very built up area (like my own in London). Certainly nobody would give it a second's thought in an area like our Mahalla, and no permission would be needed. It always sends dogs nuts, I am afraid. My cats were pretty shocked too.

I will see if in future we can do the pyrotechnics a bit earlier, and perhaps more usefully I will warn you so you can prepare the children. I should note that I have had lots of reaction from Uzbeks, including the Mahalla committee, who love the fireworks. It's one of those balance of liberties things.

Many thanks for your kind words on my general work.

Craig

I hadn't expected to receive a reply from Craig Murray, let alone one so gracious and funny. He was a busy, high-ranking diplomat, and a controversial one at that. His advocacy of human rights in Uzbekistan had rankled President Karimov. His outspokenness had also ruffled the usually staid British Foreign Office, as did his lifestyle: Murray liked to drink and socialize in bars; he had been treated for depression and had other medical problems; he was having an affair with a young Uzbek woman, Nodira Alieva, which contributed to the breakup of his marriage. The Foreign Office eventually would remove Murray from his post.

After receiving his email, I decided to invite Craig Murray over for dinner. His email made me think I'd like him. And we were, after all, neighbors. He accepted, and came to visit one Tuesday evening with his girlfriend, Nodira.

The two of them hiked over from the British ambassadorial residence, about a ten-minute walk. They were entirely alone, unaccompanied by security guards. My wife, a United Nations official, had hired extra security guards for the dinner, cognizant of the difficult nature of Murray's situation, and of reports that he had received threats against his life.

"I don't take any security measures at all," Murray said. "The problem is that it puts up a barrier between you and the people and they won't tell you what they think."

Murray didn't eat much that evening – he apologetically explained he was suffering from "Tashkent tummy," a gastro-intestinal malady that most expats experienced from time to time. But for three hours, over a few bites of chicken and glasses of red wine and green tea, Craig Murray spoke about his work and about himself.

His two years in Uzbekistan had been difficult, he said: "Probably the longest two years of my life. I'm told it is a nice place to live but a dreadful place to work. You don't feel you're getting anywhere or doing anything to help change anything, which is something I'm not used to."

Murray had previously served in Africa, in tough places like Sierra Leone. Uzbekistan, he said, was suffering from the same kind of post-colonial dysfunction that Africa had suffered after the British relinquished control.

"Uzbekistan is a Russian colony which the Russians have left and is now making essentially the same mistakes that African countries made when they were post-independent." Government control is excessive, he said, as is corruption. And the pre-existing infrastructure is falling apart. "I'm not claiming that the Soviet Union was a wonderful institution," he said. "But a key point is that what infrastructure was left after colonial times has decayed, disappeared. You know, Africa now is poorer than it was ten years ago; ten years ago it was poorer than it was twenty years ago. In absolute terms, not just in relative terms. And that's going to happen here. In ten years' time it is going to be poorer than it is now."

What follows is a transcript of some of our conversation. I asked Murray first about public opinion and Karimov. When I moved to Uzbekistan three years before, I said, people on the streets of Tashkent were largely supportive of the Uzbek leader. "Papa, he's a good guy. He makes things safe here." Especially after 9/11. That is what they told me. Now, I said, things have changed. In discussions with neighbors, or with taxi drivers or friends, I heard complaints. People complained that they were increasingly poor. They complained that Karimov is "greedy" – that's the word one man used. I asked Murray what his experience has been.

C.M.: I think that's that's absolutely right. I think all the anecdotal evidence – and that's all we have – all the evidence we have points exactly that way. I think it's the economy that's done it. It has nothing to do with human rights or authoritarianism or freedom of speech or any of those things. It's about the people who are getting poorer and poorer. And they can see their president getting richer and richer. I think there's biting poverty here. Some people in Tashkent are actually starving. It's not that Tashkent is actually starving. But for families who always had a television, the television breaks and they can't afford to get a new one. The difference between being a television owner and not a television owner makes quite a major social difference to family habits and routines. The same for refrigerators and [other] consumer [items]. Ownership of that kind of poverty is increasing in scope. It's reaching families in a way it didn't before, for many of what you might call the middle class.

R.R.: By contrast, a few months ago I went with some American Peace Corps volunteers to a *kishlak*, a rural village. I wanted to see what life was like outside of Tashkent. Everybody says Uzbekistan is not Tashkent. So I wanted to get into the provinces. So I visited this village and I guess by microeconomic standards it was poor – eighty per cent of the village didn't have water. Not everybody had electricity. I spoke with a lot of people there and didn't hear a single complaint. It seemed as if they lived their entire lives in the village and didn't know anything else, anything better. This was their life and people were optimistic. They made do. They were basically satisfied, and this struck me. Can you tell me some poverty stories from your travels, anything you have seen in villages outside of Tashkent to illustrate where Uzbekistan is right now?

C.M.: The most disillusioning case I've dealt with was in a village called Kitab, down in Kashkadarya near Shakhrisabz. And there were some private farmers there who rented land off the kolkhoz and who hadn't fulfilled their quota of apples they were supposed to produce. They were supposed to produce apples. They aren't really private farmers at all, because they're told what they have to sell, how much they have to sell, to whom and at what price. So the extent of private enterprise is extremely limited. They hadn't produced as many apples as they had been told to produce, or they had sold some privately as opposed to the kolkhoz. As a result of which one daughter had been jailed and another daughter was underground. And the mother of the family, who was eighty years old, had been beaten up. All of which is very horrible.

So I went down and visited [Kitab] and it was intensely depressing, because one thing the kolkhoz had done as a kind of punishment was to cut down all the apple trees. The entire orchard was

devastated. Hundreds of apple trees had been cut dow
awful waste. This was punishment, part of the puni
the family.

This was a terribly poor village. All the workers on this kolkhoz got two dollars a month. And, again, there was little or no electricity in the village. Little or no piped water.

So I have been trying to determine who had actually chopped down the trees. The family said the kolkhoz did. I said, yes, but, physically, who did it? Someone has chopped down hundreds of trees. Who did it? And they said actually it was their neighbors and other people in the village and even some relatives of theirs. And I said, "Why?" I mean with the kolkhoz treating this family so terribly, why was there no community solidarity against this? And they said basically the kolkhoz paid them to do this. I think it was twelve hundred soum each [about US$1.20] to chop the trees down. So the twelve-hundred-soum people were paid to chop down the fruit trees of their neighbors. And some of these people were even related to the family whose fruit trees they were chopping down. It was a kind of total lack of any feeling of what you might call horizontal solidarity. It all goes up and down to the power structure. The idea that your neighbor is having a dispute and maybe you should support him doesn't exist. There's no sense of community at all.

R.R.: There's no sense of community out of a feeling of fear? Or desperation? Did they need the soum to get by?

C.M.: Partly that. Partly a total lack of empathy I suppose. And imagination. They just can't imagine doing anything other than what the kolkhoz tells them. The order is not challenged. It is not thought that there is an alternative.

R.R.: You have been here a bit more than two years. What was the most difficult moment for you with your work as ambassador, and your most encouraging and uplifting moment?

C.M.: The lowest moment I think was that trip to Kitab, and it left me feeling totally desperate that all these people's neighbors were prepared to devastate that family because they were told to do it. What can you do? I got so cross that I stood on what would have been a village green if it was England and the entire village had turned out to see who this strange foreigner was who was wandering around. I kind of harangued them. I said, "Why did you do this? Why did you cut these trees down? These are apple trees that produce fruit. How can you destroy this? How can you do this to these people?" But it was a cry of despair. They all just looked at me with a kind of sullen resentment. No one responded. I had an interpreter. That was a low point I think. The whole situation was so damn impossible.

It's not a low point or a high point, but the point that really started me up and led directly to that speech I made on 17 October two years ago was I went to the trial of a guy called [Iskander] Khudoberganov. He had been accused with about six others of murder and robbery, basically to fund terrorism. And they were also accused of terrorism and anti-constitutional acts. I attended just one day of the trial. It was a show trial in every sense. And the evidence was farcical. There were six defendants. There was a huge charge list, but not all six were accused of all the charges. There was one particular robbery that three of them had been accused of. And the guy who had allegedly been robbed came into court. He was obviously terrified of the defendants. And the judge said to him, "Can you identify the three people who robbed you?" And he identified three people of the six who were sitting on the bench in the cage. And he managed to identify the wrong three. And the odds against that, numerically, were pretty high. And so the judge said, "No no no no no." Then the judge named the three who were meant to be identified and they stood up. And the judge said, "It was them, wasn't it?" "Oh, yes it was them." And the judge said, "Let the record show that the three were identified." The whole trial was in that kind of farcical mode.

But not only that. The judge and the prosecution were leading all the witnesses to bring Osama bin Laden's name into it at any possible point. They'd say, "They had long beards and they looked like Muslims and they talked a lot about Osama bin Laden." Or "He told me he'd been to Afghanistan to see Osama bin Laden." And there was this desperate desire to tie up Osama bin Laden into it. And it was all part of this idea that what's going on here against Muslims is part of the war against terrorism. And at the end of it these people were sentenced to death.

I won't forget this man Khudoberganov, who's twenty-one or twenty-two. I was sitting there in my suit looking out of place in this cramped courtroom, and he was looking at me with a sort of desperate appeal in his eyes, thinking, "I might not be going to die. Here is someone important in a suit and he's sitting with my family. Maybe he can save me." He was in a cage. We were only ten feet apart. And he was looking me in the eye with a sort of mute desperate plea for help. And of course there was nothing I could actually do to help. But that was the moment really when I thought, "Christ, this is awful! I've got to do something about it." People like him aren't being killed in our name. You know, we don't accept this as part of the war on terror.

R.R.: And what happened to him?

C.M.: In the end, I didn't leave it there. I went up and worked like mad on it. The European Union made a démarche to the Uzbeks. We took it to the United Nations committee on the death penalty. And currently the death penalty on him is suspended pending investigation by the UN. It doesn't mean he won't be executed. I mean this year they executed people in his situation while there's a UN investigation going on. But they have said in his case they won't. So I've got no doubt at all that my personal instigation helped get that death penalty stopped.

R.R.: Let's talk about the police in Uzbekistan. The police presence struck me here. Cops are standing every fifty yards in some places. What's your take on the police and their role in society?

C.M.: It's quite extraordinary. There are forty thousand police in Tashkent alone. There are also non-uniformed police, SNB [state security] operatives. In terms of people in the capital who actually have a job, it's probably thirty per cent. Which is really quite extraordinary.

R.R.: The largest employer in the city?

C.M.: Yeah yeah. Effectively it's a police state. One of the things that interests me is the amount of casual rape that goes on by the police. There have been several girls who have been raped by the police.

R.R.: How do you know that?

C.M.: They've told me. The girls have told me. And it's not at all unusual. And there's nothing you can do about it. And in a couple of cases I said, "Well, why didn't you tell me at the time?" and they said, "What good is it going to do anyway?"

That's just one example of abuse. And there's also extorting people. You know, for not having a license for the bazaar, or not having the kind of traffic documents or whatever.

One interesting thing about the big roundup of people after the March bombings: lots of people were arrested and there's an absolute minimum of seven hundred still held; they kind of fall into two groups. There are people who are connected to the opposition, who are connected to Muslim movements, or who are particularly religious. And a huge amount of people, at least here in Tashkent, were arrested simply because they're fairly wealthy, in an attempt to get money from them. I'm including a couple of employees of the British Council who were taken. I had five or six people who have come to see me personally who were either personally a victim of this or were, say, the parents of victims of this, where people were just taken up and told, "You have to pay over." In the case of a British Council employee, it was five thousand dollars he had to pay, and he was released. He, in order to get released, had signed a document implicating someone else from a wealthier family, from whom the police were asking twenty thousand dollars.

R.R.: Let me ask you about the March bombings. The thing that struck me most about that was the reaction of people I spoke to. Again, totally anecdotal, but there was a consistency. Which was, I wouldn't say sympathy necessarily with the terrorists, the people who did the bombing, but there was no sympathy for the police victims. It was like "Too bad they didn't get another cop." Is that what you heard as well?

C.M.: Yes, I agree with that. They had it coming. That was the general reaction. Look, in the ordinary population I don't know that anyone condemned the bombing, among normal people. And I found that when I was talking about it with ordinary Uzbeks, when, I would normally say, "Of course we condemn violence, these are stupid acts of violence, but we understand how desperate people get led into this by the terrible situation; you have to look at the causes, but the acts of violence themselves must be condemned." You can sense from an audience whether you've got their sympathy or not, and when I was condemning the violence, doing that bit, I plainly hadn't got sympathy in my audience, be they journalists or democratic activists, whomever I was speaking to. And this was an educated part of the population, and among the less educated it really was "No they deserved it. They had it coming. We wish they had got some more."

R.R.: We were talking earlier about Karimov. What's your take on how powerful he is? There are two schools of thought – one, that he's all powerful, and, two, that he's not, that he's controlled by others.

C.M.: I think he's extremely powerful. I tend more to the all-powerful than to the spokesman-for-the-collective school of thought.

R.R.: Have you ever met him?

C.M.: Yeah.

R.R.: On more than one occasion?

C.M.: Yeah.

R.R.: Does he talk to you?

C.M.: Yeah. Strangely, when we're at something where there are quite a lot of people, he almost always makes a point of coming up to me and ostentatiously shaking my hand, thus ignoring all the ambassadors who for some peculiar reason would like to shake his hand. And annoying me, because I don't want to. [Murray laughs loudly.] He manages to [upset] everyone all at the same time, which is quite amazing.

R.R.: Have you had private meetings with him?

C.M.: Uh huh.

R.R.: What's your take of the man?

C.M.: Extremely intelligent. Very, very, very bright. Very well briefed. Very cunning. He knows immediately how to find weak points. Before I ever said anything to him the very first words he ever said to me were that he understood that, because of September 11 and the need to fight against terror, Britain had just opted out of certain clauses of the European Convention on Human Rights, which is kind of a preemptive strike against me saying anything to him about the Uzbek stance (on human rights), and that's smart. I mean, it had only just happened. It was quite an obscure item in the British news. Only sort of liberal intellectuals would have picked up on it on page twenty-two of their newspapers. It's a very good, bright opening salvo. He's shrewd; he's well informed, very well informed. But he operates within strict confines and doesn't have a large idea of the world. His world view is more paranoid. He's seen the Soviet system, which he understood and grew up in, collapse, and he's gotten independence he never really wanted and he's trying to use it to maintain the Soviet system in one small country.

R.R.: Have you met his daughters?

C.M.: Yeah, both of them.

R.R.: What do you make of Gulnora, the business tycoon?

C.M.: Gulnora, when you meet her, is very charming, very girlish, very pleasant, amusing. She came along to the Queen's birthday party two years ago and we were chatting away about nothing in particular. And a drunk came up. This chap was the Deputy Khokim [Governor] of Navoi. And he staggered up to me and said, "I need to speak with you." And I said, "Okay, not now I'm busy, in ten minutes." And she was there completely incognito. She was elegantly dressed. Quite tall, striking figure. But she had no body-guards; she had nothing around to show she was the President's daughter. So I said to him in my very bad Russian, "Ya ochen zanyat. Cherez desyat minut." ["I'm very busy. I'll see you in ten minutes."] At any rate he said, "No, I need to speak to you now." And he pushed her on the shoulder and said, "Hey, you're an interpreter, right?" And she said nothing at all. While she might have said "No, I'm not an interpreter," or something along those lines, she didn't say anything. And so he pushed her again a second time, really very roughly, and said, "No, but you can interpret. Interpret for me now." I sort of put my arm around him and led him away.

R.R.: He didn't know who she was.

C.M.: He didn't know who she was. And, strangely, I've never seen him since. What happened to him I don't know. But at the time, as he disappeared off, I came back – I dumped him on the South African consul – I went back to her and said, "Look, I'm terribly sorry." She giggled and said, "That's quite okay." She said, "Do you think I could get a job as your interpreter?" [Murray laughs loudly, a belly laugh.] Which was really very nice. When you meet her, strangely, despite all the terrible things you know about her – she's funny, girlish, witty, very approachable, and very nice. Kind of completely not what you would expect.

R.R.: Nobody can predict the future, but, as a guy who has spent his career working on Russian affairs, intuitively I feel that at some point in this country, pardon my language, but the shit is going to hit the fan and Karimov's going to go. What's your sense of what's going to happen?

C.M.: I think that's right. I don't think it's close. It's four or five years away. Obviously it's quite dangerous. Everyone's getting poorer. There's no democratic outlet.

R.R.: No safety valve.

C.M.: Exactly. So they're going to extremism. They don't see a liberal alternative. They're not aware of a liberal alternative. One thing that really depresses me is, most Uzbeks figure what they have now is capitalism and democracy. This is what Karimov tells them all the time, that we are a democratic, capitalist state. And people believe that because they don't know what one is, because they've got no other sources of information. Lots of Uzbeks say to me, "I don't think much of this capitalism and democracy we've got now. The Soviet Union was much better. We can't go back to that. Maybe a caliphate would be better." You have to go back to basics and explain to them why this isn't a democracy, why this isn't capitalism. But their lack of information is really desperate, and that's really scary, the depth of ignorance about the outside world.

R.R.: Is there any hope at all? Do you see anyone within the government structure who might be able to turn things around?

C.M.: I've spoken to, say, people just below the top, not far below the top, in institutions like the central bank. Really, people in their twenties in quite senior positions. And if you ask them what do you need to do in society, they'd give you the same prescription for the economy that I would. They understand. They've been educated in London or whatever, and they're fine. But the trouble is they're forty years away from physical [sic] power, and they'll never get higher than being the number three or four in the bank until a lot of old people die. I think there's no doubt that there's a generation of very capable Western-educated, largely young Uzbeks in their twenties or early thirties. And what they need to do is what Eastern Europe did, which is they basically scrapped a generation and only had almost totally young ministers and senior officials in the early nineties. [But here] the Soviet gerontocracy idea is still in charge.

R.R.: What's your prescription? How do you cure Uzbekistan?

C.M.: I think you've got to just get rid of the present leadership entirely. Lock, stock, and barrel. I don't see any other way that it's going to go forward at all.

R.R.: And replace them with whom?

C.M.: Much younger. Much younger people.

R.R.: That's not a realistic prescription.

C.M.: It's not going to happen. If you want to cure Uzbekistan it's like saying there is a medicine that exists, but you can't afford it, you can't get hold of it. It's not going to happen.

R.R.: So when you report to the Foreign Office and take an educated guess as to where things are headed here, what do you say?

C.M.: I say it's heading for disaster. This place is heading towards a failed state. It's heading for a disastrous scenario with increasing poverty, despair, leading to a cycle of increased oppression to try and keep the lid on it all, and eventual explosion probably, eventually an Islamic direction, and that's where it's going. Unless something radical happens to change it. But what that radical thing could be is very hard to say. That's where I see it going.

R.R.: Do you like your job? You said yourself this has been a tough, really difficult two years for you. You've had the opportunity to leave. Anybody can leave. Why do you continue to do it?

C.M.: I think, it's very difficult to say it without sounding awfully cheesy, but it's basically kind of a moral commitment. I've taken it on and I've got to see it through. I've pointed out things here that wouldn't have got pointed out were I not here. And that has made a difference to the course of events and I can keep making a difference to the course of events. I actually do go with human-rights activists when they're called in for interrogation. I sort of turn up with them and sometimes that can mean that they don't get tortured as they might have been otherwise. And even at that kind of tiny personal level you can make a difference. And frankly anyone who replaces me isn't going to do that.

At this point in our conversation, my wife, Eriko, and Murray's girlfriend, Nodira, joined the conversation.

Eriko: For the British foreign service, Central Asia means a lot. I'm reading this book called *The Great Game,* and I finally understood why the British, unlike Americans, who don't know where Uzbekistan is – have a great interest in what happens here. It seems like the British have this intellectual interest. Did that kind of historical background actually affect you when you came here? Did you think about that?

C.M.: Absolutely a hundred per cent. Yeah. I just leapt at the chance to come here. I studied imperial history anyway at the university. From the point of view of the nineteenth century and the Great Game and Uzbekistan and all this region as seen by the Russians or as seen by the UK, I knew a huge amount. What I didn't know of course was Uzbekistan as seen by the Uzbeks, which is a different question. Absolutely, the idea that I was following in the footsteps of [the great British adventurers] Alexander Burnes and [Charles] Stoddart and [Arthur] Conolly and all those people, very very much. The other thing is, we're sitting here in a place where you couldn't go, where British people certainly couldn't go. If you look at the British people who came here prior to the Russian invasion, you could almost count them on the fingers of two hands. Like Stoddart and Conolly – they died, the two of them got executed – and Alexander Burnes was murdered in Kabul. You know, it was very very few people who came at all. A tiny number. Then between the Russian conquest in 1870 or whenever it was and 1914, it was closed to British nationals by the Russian government. Then of course it was closed by the Soviets. In history, the number of British people who have been able to come here is probably less than a couple of thousand. So it's absolutely amazing to be here in that sense. I think about that. Or I did. I kind of lost sight of it. And Samarkand, of course, in British literature is a kind of mythical place. Tamerlane, you know, is a play by Marlowe. To actually see

[Tamerlane's] grave, where he's buried, is quite extraordinary. I don't know why it's so extraordinary because you can go see the grave of his contemporary, say Henry III in England, and no one thinks that's strange at all. You expect him to have a grave. But somehow Tamerlane is more mythical to us than Henry III.

I asked Nodira, who was in her twenties, about Tamerlane – Amir Timur – whether, in a broad sense, she and those of her generation considered themselves to be Tamerlane's children. Her cell phone rang. It was her mother. Nodira asked her the question. The mother hung up. "I think Tamerlane had four children," Nodira said. "That's what I told my mom."

"I didn't mean it literally," I said. "I meant do you, as a young Uzbek woman, feel a connection to Amir Timur?"

"You mean now?" she asks.

"Yes. He's your national hero."

"No, our father is Islam Karimov."

"Ah, Papa," I said.

"Papa."

"But what about Amir Timur?"

Nodira paused. "Have you been to the Amir Timur museum? He was great – how can I say in English – a great fighter. I never heard that we called him father. We call him great fighter. And national hero."

"A good choice?" I asked.

"Yes," Nodira said. "I'm proud of Amir Timur. I'm proud. We've been taught a lot about him, so I'm proud. How about you? Is there something wrong, because you're asking these questions? These are real unusual questions. But you know in Soviet times we were taught that he was a killer."

Craig Murray interjected, "Well, he was."

"But Craig," Nodira said, "if he was not a killer, how could he achieve all these things?"

Nodira's cell phone rang again. She retired to a corner of the living room to talk. Ambassador Murray listened in. "Nodira's mom is explaining more to her about Amir Timur," he said.

Nodira returned to the dinner table. "My mom says one of Amir Timur's sons was an alcoholic. I asked my mom. I said, 'Mom, Amir Timur had four children?' She said, 'I don't know. I will ask your dad.' I said, 'Okay, it doesn't matter. I think it was four.' But she called back and said, 'Yeah, you were right, it was four. One of them was an alcoholic!'"

Everybody laughed.

Andijon

May 2005 began inauspiciously in Tashkent. A group of several dozen rural Uzbeks had traveled to the capital from Shahrisabz, fifty miles south of Samarkand. Shahrisabz was Amir Timur's birthplace. The travelers had come to stage a protest. Many of them were relatives of a farmer whose land the local authorities had seized – illegally, the protesters said – in 2001.

On the morning of Tuesday, 3 May, the demonstrators, in a bold and unprecedented action, set up tents outside the US Embassy, hoping to press their demand that the farmer's land be returned. Some of the protesters carried placards calling for the resignation of Uzbek government officials and for an end to poverty. They figured that if their action failed, the Americans, who doubtless would be monitoring the proceedings, might grant them political asylum.

The Uzbek authorities were on edge. In March 2005, a largely peaceful popular revolution had toppled the regime of Askar Akayev in neighboring Kyrgyzstan. Before that, democratic rebellions had changed the governments of Ukraine and Georgia. Many wondered whether Uzbekistan was next.

Late on the evening of 3 May, Uzbek police assaulted the demonstrators, with whom they briefly had clashed earlier in the day. One eyewitness described what happened: "Two buses full of Interior Ministry officers arrived and started beating protesters, including both men and women, with truncheons. In tents set up outside the embassy, there were little children, including nine- and ten-month-old babies. Many policemen stamped on those tents. There were little children asleep there. I don't know what happened to them. Almost all [the protesters] seemed to be injured. Their noses and mouths were bleeding. They were forced into buses that departed in an unknown direction."[72]

Another eyewitness said the protesters were "trembling with fear." "The demonstrators were so intimidated that they put their hands in the air and called out that they would stop their protest action and go home immediately. Their pleas were ignored and the security forces waded in, beating people apparently indiscriminately."[73]

The US Embassy issued a statement the next day. "The demonstrators who had set up a camp across the street from the US Embassy on 3 May were exercising their right to freedom of expression and assembly that are recognized by the United Nations Universal Declaration of Human Rights," the statement said. "They posed no threat to embassy security, nor did they interfere with the embassy's operations in any way. We regret that government authorities overnight removed them and resorted to force to do so."[74]

Thus began Uzbekistan's summer of troubles, which would end with a major rift in US–Uzbek relations and the expulsion of America from its post-9/11 military base in Karshi-Khanabad.

The flashpoint was a place in northeastern Uzbekistan called Andijon, in the Ferghana Valley. Andijon is Uzbekistan's fourth-largest city. On 10 May, twenty-three Muslim businessmen were put on trial there, accused of religious extremism and links to terrorism. Human-rights groups claimed the charges were false and alleged the trial was a politically motivated effort by the government targeting entrepreneurs.[75]

The trial generated some public protests in Andijon as supporters of the defendants gathered near the courthouse. On Thursday night, 12 May, armed men stormed the prison where the defendants were being held, and also took over a military garrison. Weapons were seized and several thousand prisoners, including the defendants, were released.

The US Embassy in Tashkent also reported "that a suicide bomber was shot outside of the Israeli Embassy" on the morning of Friday, 13 May. In a message distributed to Americans in Uzbekistan, the US said it had received "reports of gunfire and possible explosions" in Andijon and urged its citizens "to stay off the streets."

In Andijon, events spiraled out of control. President Karimov rushed to the city. Andijon residents gathered in the streets and in the town's central square. What had begun as a prison assault turned into a popular uprising. Loudspeakers were set up, and citizens demanded economic and political reform.

"The nation has been tortured by the totalitarian regime of President Karimov and by corruption at all levels of the state," one man told the crowd. "The people demand justice, freedom and democracy."[76]

Rumors spread that Karimov would come to address the demonstrators, whose numbers swelled. Late that Friday afternoon, a government helicopter swooped over the main square. The early evening sky darkened with rain clouds. Vehicles with heavy machineguns and armed soldiers rushed in. "From the sky there was a storm of rain, from the streets a storm of bullets," one eyewitness recalled.[77] Hundreds of people – as many as five hundred – were reported to have been killed. The event came to be called the "Andijon massacre" and "bloody Friday."[78]

Karimov blamed the violence on Islamic militants and claimed "no one ordered [troops] to fire" at the demonstrators.[79] The events in Andijon "were clearly an attempt to reproduce what happened in Kyrgyzstan in recent months," Karimov said. "Suppressed fundamentalist groups in Andijon tried to carry out their plans formulated over a long time. They hoped that weak local and central power would allow a Kyrgyz variant. Calling on youth with poisoned ideas, they counted on achieving their goals by seizing administrative buildings, overthrowing the authorities constitutionally chosen by the people, and creating a Muslim caliphate here."[80]

Uzbekistan's Procurator, Rashid Kadyrov, said, "only terrorists were liquidated by government forces," and claimed, "not a single civilian was killed by government forces" in Andijon.[81] Eyewitness accounts proved this assertion to be false. The UN's Human Rights Commissioner, Louise Arbour, would describe the carnage as, "a mass killing."

In the hours and days after the violence, hundreds of Uzbeks fled Andijon for nearby Kyrgyzstan, where they became refugees under the protection of the United Nations High Commissioner for Refugees (UNHCR). The international community, including the United States, condemned the Uzbek government's handling of the Andijon crisis and called for a thorough, internationally sponsored inquiry.

"It's becoming increasingly clear that very large numbers of civilians were killed by the indiscriminate use of force by Uzbek forces," State Department spokesman Richard Boucher said. "There needs to be a credible and a transparent accounting to establish the facts of the matter of what occurred in Andijon."

"At the same time," Boucher said, "I think it's clear that the episode began by an armed attack on the prison and on other government facilities. There are reports of hostage-taking and other claims that should be investigated. Nothing justified such acts of violence."[82]

Secretary of State Condoleezza Rice called on Uzbekistan to embrace reform, and said that, despite Washington's friendship with Tashkent, "the United States held all countries equally responsible to engage in human rights practices that are sound and to engage in processes of democracy and democratization and openness."[83]

Uzbekistan rejected these calls. In the weeks after Andijon, relations between Tashkent and Washington deteriorated. The US Peace Corps suspended its program in Uzbekistan after the Uzbeks refused to renew the visas of fifty-two volunteers.[84] The US and Israel temporarily ordered nonessential diplomatic personnel and family members to leave Uzbekistan, citing information that Islamic terrorist groups were planning new attacks.[85] An Uzbek Foreign Ministry official deplored the American and Israeli move, calling it "none other than the continuation of the information war against Uzbekistan [and] an attempt to show that instability might form in Uzbekistan."[86]

President Karimov displayed increasing irritation with Western, and in particular American, calls for an independent probe of the Andijon violence. George Bloch, an American, was the United Nations field security coordination officer in Tashkent at the time. He attended a briefing by Karimov.

"I was sitting right in front of him," Bloch told me. "I later learned US diplomats had just visited him at his house and delivered a harsh message about what Uzbekistan was supposed to do. You could tell he was personally furious at this whole thing."

Bloch was among the political casualties of Andijon, a victim, he said, of Uzbekistan's irritation with the US. "The Uzbeks warned the UN that I should be reassigned," Bloch said. He said the Uzbeks accused him, falsely, of being a spy for the Americans. At the request of the UN, Bloch left the country on 17 July.

Bloch gives credence to Karimov's assertion that the Andijon events were sparked by Islamic militants. "There was no question in my mind, and at the American embassy, and in the CIA's mind, and in the Israelis', and in the Russians' mind that these radical Islamic networks did have something to do with the *original* events, which was the attack upon a prison and a police barracks and an armory. This was not something that was organized by the prisoners' relatives. The Uzbeks said 150 people were involved in the attacks. I don't know if that is correct, but even if you had twenty guys with guns, that's a pretty significant number in Uzbekistan. So we were all convinced that these radical networks had something to do with the planning and organization of the attacks."

Within weeks of the Andijon events, Uzbekistan's foreign policy gaze shifted away from the US and towards America's rivals in Central Asia. Karimov traveled to China and to Russia, where he was warmly and uncritically received.[87] In June, Russia's Defense Minister announced in Tashkent that Uzbek and Russian military forces would hold joint maneuvers, the first since the fall of the Soviet Union.[88] At the end of July, Uzbekistan ordered the US to leave the Karshi-Khanabad military base within six months.[89] The eviction notice was delivered after the United States applauded – and Uzbekistan opposed – UNHCR's transfer of 439 Andijon refugees from Kyrgyzstan to Romania on 29 July.

"By providing sanctuary for the asylum seekers and allowing today's humanitarian transfer," a US State Department spokesman said, "the Kyrgyz Republic has demonstrated its commitment to support international efforts to assist individuals who seek protection from persecution. The Kyrgyz Republic deserves the thanks of all those in the international community who are committed to the UN's humanitarian principles."[90]

American officials played down the loss of K-2, which had helped to anchor post-9/11 US military operations in Afghanistan. Even before the eviction, Pentagon spokesman Lawrence Di Rita described the base as not "critical." "There's no single installation anywhere in the world that we must have and can't live without."[91] The US maintains a military facility in Kyrgyzstan, and Defense Secretary Donald Rumsfeld visited Kyrgyzstan and Tajikistan in late July 2005, where he received support for America's continued presence in Central Asia.[92] Rumsfeld pointedly did not stop off in Tashkent on that trip.

Epilogue

What's next in Uzbekistan? George Bloch, the former head of UN security in Tashkent, told me the following story when I posed that question to him, several months after Andijon.

"Uzbekistan," he said, "is on this horrible slide downhill. Everybody knows it." That was his view, he said. And the view of a top Uzbek official he had recently encountered. "This was a guy who had been a senior member of the Ministry of Interior counter-terrorist unit, and he approached me saying exactly these kind of things. He was a useful contact, for he would provide us with information, like crime statistics. This was a guy who was going into retirement but who had been a senior figure for a long time and had known Karimov in his youth. And he had no hesitation to say how bad things were, how the country was going downhill."

Bloch shares the view expressed by Craig Murray that Uzbekistan may be headed towards disaster. "A failed state" is how they both put it. What kind of failed state? I cannot say for sure whether they meant it figuratively – a viable but sickly state that is unable to provide the basic necessities for its citizens – or literally: the breakup of Uzbekistan. It is not too far-fetched, I think, to argue that some of Uzbekistan's constituent parts, in a worst-case scenario of total chaos, could attempt to go their own way: the Ferghana Valley as some sort of Islamic entity; Karakalpakstan as an independent entity; elsewhere, some sort of crisis-driven hunkering down by clans (Samarkand, Tashkent) or ethnicity (there are significant numbers of Tajiks in Bukhara, for instance). I personally do not foresee the breakup of post-Soviet Uzbekistan per se. I do envision a continuing crisis and a bleak future.

It would be tempting to hope that Uzbekistan, especially after the events in Andijon, might hop onto the wave of democracy that has washed over many former Soviet republics: Ukraine, Georgia, Kyrgyzstan (maybe). But Uzbekistan, as I've written, has never been a gentle place. The outcome of violence in Andijon will be more instability, and perhaps a regime change in which one authoritarian boss replaces another.

President Islam Karimov is a leader who values power. He's the former Communist Party chief and the first and only president of an independent Uzbekistan. On the street they call him "Papa." Those who like him do so kindly. Those who do not, and there are many of them, use the moniker in the pejorative, as in Mafia "Godfather."

A cult of personality envelops the man. Students are required to study Karimov's prose. His picture occupies prominent places. Recall my visit to the office of the Mufti, the state-appointed

Islamic leader of Uzbekistan. A life-size-times-two Karimov portrait hovers over the cleric's desk.

Karimov last ran for office in 2000. His opponent announced that he himself had voted for Karimov as the better man. In 2002, in an election the State Department called "neither free nor fair," Uzbek citizens overwhelmingly approved a referendum to extend Karimov's term from five to seven years. A friend of mine, a resident of Tashkent, told me how government flacks had come to his apartment building in advance of the vote, asking residents whether they were intending to support the President. My friend, who abhorred Karimov and opposed the ballot initiative, kept silent and, wholly intimidated, refrained from voting altogether. "I am afraid to vote no," he said. "Who knows what might happen to me?"

The short-lived popular uprising in Andijon notwithstanding, there is no democratic alternative to Karimov. What lies ahead is trouble. There is no viable opposition party in Uzbekistan. There is no free speech. There is no free press. What moves events there are powerful, competing interests – clans – and the interplay of clan interests is likely to decide how the future will play out.

The two most powerful clans are from Samarkand and Tashkent. Its members are a soup of business and political associates, many related, who share a common interest in accumulating and preserving economic and political power. Analysts of Uzbek politics will tell you that the Tashkent clan is led by Rustam Inoyatov, head of Uzbekistan's National Security Council. These are the state security guys, the former KGB. The Samarkand clan has been led by Zakir Almatov, leader of the Ministry of Internal Affairs, also known as the police. Both organizations are, by nature of their work, armed and dangerous. Islam Karimov, though from Samarkand, is said to play one man, and one clan, against the other.

Things turned interesting in December 2005, when Almatov resigned, honorably it seems, because of poor health. This may enhance Karimov's control over the Samarkand clan, and there-fore strengthen his position – or the position of his clan – vis-a-vis Inoyatov in any succession struggle.

In any case, clan-based politics is a tricky game. If events in Uzbekistan further appear to spiral out of control, some form of clan-led palace revolt could engineer Karimov's ouster in the name of ending the violence or of restoring stability. It all could be done, ostensibly and cynically, in the name of democratic reform. A most likely scenario would see Inoyatov leading the charge. With the retirement of Almatov, he appears to be the only player strong enough to bring about such dramatic political change. Inoyatov could potentially be joined by a disgruntled faction within Karimov's own Samarkand clan.

Whichever scenario plays out, it is clear that a new regime is not likely to come from the streets, as it did in Kiev or in Tblisi, because the streets of Tashkent literally are lined with police, and regime opponents – leaders to rally the masses – have effectively been snuffed out. There will not be a Velvet or Orange Revolution in Uzbekistan.

Nor will a new regime come from the ballot box. Presidential elections are scheduled for 2007. Whether Karimov runs again or not, there are no viable opposition political parties in Uzbekistan. Karimov will win, or his hand-picked successor will. Violence and acts of terror are real possibilities as the election approaches.

Karimov will eventually exit, but what comes next won't be a whole lot better, and may even be worse.

Notes

1. *Islam Karimov. The First President of the Republic of Uzbekistan* (Tashkent: Vilartes & Leppelt, 1998).
2. United Nations Development Programme, *Human Development Report 2003* (New York: Oxford University Press, 2003), p. 53.
3. *Washington Post,* 9 October 2001.
4. Article 158 of the Criminal Code of Uzbekistan reads, "Public insult or slander towards the President of Uzbekistan, as well as by using the press or other mass media shall be punished by correctional labor up to three years or arrest up to six months, or by five years of imprisonment."
5. See Peter Hopkirk, *The Great Game: The Struggle for Empire in Central Asia* (New York: Kodansha America, 1994).
6. James Baker, testifying on 24 February 1992 before the Subcommittee on Foreign Operations of the House Appropriations Committee, Washington, <http://dosfan.lib.uic.edu/ERC/briefing/ dispatch/1992/ html/Dispatchv3no08.html>.
7. *Christian Science Monitor,* 14 August 1998.

8. See Lyle J. Goldstein, "Making the Most of Central Asian Partnerships," *Joint Force Quarterly*, Summer 2002, <http://www.findarticles.com/p/articles/mi_m0KNN/is_2002_Summer/ai_99817516>.

9. C. J. Chivers, "Long before War, Green Berets Built Military Ties to Uzbekistan," *New York Times*, 25 October 2001.

10. See Svante E. Cornell, "Uzbekistan: A Regional Player in Eurasian Geopolitics?" *European Security*, 9(2), 2000, <http://www.cornell-caspian.com/pub/0010uzbekistan.htm>.

11. See the prepared testimony by Martha Brill Olcott before the Subcommittee on International Economic Policy, Export and Trade Promotion of the Senate Foreign Relations Committee, 8 July 1998, <http://www.ceip.org/people/olccaspw.htm>.

12. Franks was speaking at a press conference in Tashkent on 18 May 2001. The complete text of his remarks is available at <usembassy.uz>.

13. Ambassador Herbst replied to my questions about 9/11 via email in October 2004.

14. These comments were made on *Akhborot*, the main evening news broadcast, 18 October 2001.

15. *Washington Post*, 13 October 2001.

16. *Washington Post*, 13 October 2001.

17. Reuters, 12 October 2001.

18. *Washington Post*, 13 October 2001.

19. Reuters, 12 March 2002.

20. *Washington Post*, 13 March 2002.

21. Reuters, 12 March 2002.

22. *Washington Post*, 13 March 2002.

23. *Washington Post*, 13 March 2002.

24. Associated Press, 11 March 2002, "Uzbekistan Slowly Seeing Change."

25. US Department of State, Uzbekistan Country Report on Human Rights Practices 2003, 25 February 2004, <www.state.gov/g/drl/rls/hrrpt/2003/27873pf.htm>.

26. Rachel Denber, acting executive director of Human Rights Watch's Europe and Central Asia division, press release, 14 July 2004, <www.hrw.org/english/docs/2004/07/14/uzbeki9062.htm>.

27. Karimov quotes are from A. Iriskulov, V. Ignatenko, A. Kim,

L. Skosirskeya, and S. Glasirina, eds., *Amir Temur in World History* (Tashkent: Sharq, 2001).

28. Beatrice Forbes Manz, "Tamerlane's Career and Its Uses," *Journal of World History*, 13(1), 2002, p. 4.
29. Iriskulov et al., *Amir Temur in World History*, pp. 28–30.
30. Beatrice Forbes Manz, *The Rise and Rule of Tamerlane* (Cambridge, England: Cambridge University Press, 1989).
31. Ibid., pp. 1–18.
32. Manz, "Tamerlane's Career," p. 22.
33. See UNESCO's Memory of the World Register, <www.unesco.org/webworld/mdm/1997/eng/uzbekistan/uzbekistanom.html>.
34. Huston Smith, *Islam: A Concise Introduction* (San Francisco: HarperSanFrancisco, 2001), pp. 30–31.
35. See page 3 of UNESCO's Memory of the World Register.
36. Boris Lunin, "Proiskhozhdenie i sud'ba Korana Osmana," *O'Zbekiston Tarixi*, 4, 2000, p. 26.
37. See UNESCO's Memory of the World Register.
38. Lunin, "Proiskhozhdenie i sud'ba Korana Osmana," p. 22.
39. Ibid., p. 26.
40. Hopkirk, *The Great Game*, p. 315.
41. Lunin, "Proiskhozhdenie i sud'ba Korana Osmana," p. 21.
42. Interview with Murod Gulyamov, one of the librarians in charge of the Qur'an of Othman, Tashkent, 24 June 2004.
43. Lunin, "Proiskhozhdenie i sud'ba Korana Osmana," p. 25.
44. Ibid., p. 24.
45. The document is in the Central State Archives of Uzbekistan: TsGA UzSSR, Fond No. 394, Opis' No. 1, Delo No. 37, List No. 25.
46. TsGUzSSR, Fond No. 394, Opis' No. 1, Delo No. 39, List No. 13.
47. *New York Times*, 16 August 2001.
48. See the Human Rights Watch, "Uzbekistan: Sacrificing Women to Save the Family? Domestic Violence in Uzbekistan," July 2001, Vol. 13, No. 4(D), pp. 3, 13, 15.
49. Minnesota Advocates for Human Rights, *Domestic Violence in Uzbekistan.* (Minneapolis, 2000), p. 26.
50. See "History of the Akhal-Teke," www.mhref.com.
51. Central Intelligence Agency World Factbook: Uzbekistan, <http://cia.gov/cia/publications/factbook/geos/uz.html#Econ>.
52. Ibid.

53. Interview with Dilshod Khidirov of the World Bank's Tashkent office, Tashkent, 28 November 2002.

54. A note on the UNOCD document's sources: In addition to the information gathered in the country survey, the document cites the following as sources of information for the section cited here: interviews conducted by the report's author in Tashkent, April 1997; "In Uzbekistan, Crackdown on 'Mafia' Creates Political Waves" Agence France Presse, 13 May 1993; Observatoire Geopolitique Des Drogues 1997; Usman Khaknazarov, "Renaissance of Power Broker of Uzbek Policy," 20 February 2003; Andrew Jennings, "Fraud of the Rings," *Sydney Morning Herald*, 15 July 2000; "Uzbekistan Protests Olympic Ban," *Moscow RIA* (in Russian), 12 September 2000; "Uzbekistan Protests Ban on Olympic Coach," *Uzbekistan Daily Digest*, 12 September 2000; "Uzbek Boxing Official Defamed in Book," Agence France Presse, 1 February 2000; *Intelligence Newsletter*, 23 September 1999; Paul Farrelly, Michael Gillard, and David Connett, "Lord Owen's Russian Enigma: Revealed: The Secret History of Alisher Usmanov, Moscow Lieutenant to the Former Foreign Secretary," *The Observer*, 29 November 1998; Bjorn Lambek, "Carlsberg Dealing with the Mafia," *Copenhagen Politiken* (in Danish), 19 March 1998; Vladimir Ivanidze, "Who Is Leading Them, Eh?" *Moscow Russkiy Telegraf* (in Russian), 27 August 1998, p. 6; "New Uzbek Network in Europe," *Intelligence Newsletter*, 10 June 1999.

55. See "Uzbekistan: Merchants, Consumers Paying High Price for Presidential Decrees," 1 August 2002, <www.eurasianet.org>.

56. Ibid.

57. Associated Press, 6 January 2003.

58. See Esmer Islamov and Samariddin Sharipov, "Signs Show Uzbek Stability Buckling under Economic Stress," 16 November 2004, <www.eurasianet.org>.

59. See "Uzbekistan: Merchants, Consumers Paying High Price."

60. Associated Press, 4 November 2002.

61. Islamov and Sharipov, "Signs Show Uzbek Stability Buckling."

62. The British *Financial Times* published an investigative piece on 19 August 2003 which spelled out the extent of Gulnora Karimova's holdings. In July 2004, the *Moscow Times* reported that Karimova had sold her interest in Uzdonrobita to a Moscow-based mobile-telephone company for as much as US$159 million.

63. See page 23 of the International Crisis Group report.

64. Ibid.

65. See the US Department of State's 2003 Country Report on human rights practices in Uzbekistan, February 2004, <www.state.gov>.

66. Analytical and Information Center, Ministry of Health of the Republic of Uzbekistan, State Department of Statistics, Ministry of Macroeconomics and Statistics, and ORC Macro, *Uzbekistan Health Examination Survey 2002* (Calverton, MD: Analytical and Information Center, State Department of Statistics, and ORC Macro, 2004), p. 202.

67. Ibid., pp. 210–211.

68. See the report, released on 25 February 2004, <http://www.state.gov/g/drl/rls/hrrpt/2003/27873.htm>.

69. For a write-through of the events, see Peter Baker, "Group Linked to Al Qaeda Suspected in Uzbek Unrest," *Washington Post*, 2 April 2004.

70. For a report on these bombings, see C. J. Chivers, "At Least 2 Are Killed in Coordinated Blasts at Embassies in Uzbekistan," *New York Times*, 31 July 2004.

71. See note 4.

72. Daniel Kimmage, "Uzbekistan: Police Crush Protest in Tashkent," 10 May 2005, <http://www.rferl.org/featuresarticle/2005/5/1050411F-88D7-4331-AC72-27EBD8E17B9E.html>.

73. Report by Institute for War and Peace Reporting correspondent Galima Bukharbaeva, 4 May 2005, <www.iwpr.net>.

74. <IRINNews.org>, 6 May 2005.

75. See Gulnoza Saidazimova, "Uzbekistan: Protesters Charge Officials with Using Extremism. Charges to Target Entrepreneurs," 11 May 2005, <http://www.rferl.org/featuresarticle/2005/05/8ef6fb25-fa97-4fa3-9bc6-44b185158137.html>.

76. Reuters, 13 May 2005.

77. N. C. Aizenman, "In Uzbekistan, Families Caught in a Nightmare," *Washington Post*, 18 May 2005.

78. The most comprehensive account of what happened in Andijon is contained in a report by Human Rights Watch, which concluded that Uzbek troops had unjustifiably shot unarmed people on a mass scale. See "Bullets Were Falling like Rain. The Andijan Massacre, May 13, 2005," <http://hrw.org/reports/2005/uzbekistan0605>. The

United Nations High Commissioner for Human Rights, Louise Arbour, described the shootings as "a mass killing." Citing eyewitness testimony, Arbour wrote that "grave human rights violations, mostly of the right to life, were committed by Uzbek military and security forces." See Sam Cage, "UN: Uzbek Troops to Fault in Uprising," Associated Press, 12 July 2005.

79. Reuters, 14 May 2005.

80. Karimov speaking at a press conference, 14 May 2005, <www.gov.uz>.

81. <news.bbc.co.uk>, 17 May 2005.

82. Transcript of press briefing, <www.state.gov>, 18 May 2005.

83. Associated Press, 18 May 2005.

84. Press release, <usembassy.uz>, 6 June 2005.

85. C. J. Chivers, "Israel Evacuates Staff from Uzbekistan as Instability Worsens," *New York Times*, 4 June 2005.

86. Itar-Tass, Tashkent, 6 June 2005.

87. See, for example, Henry Meyer, "Uzbekistan President Says Uprising against His Government in May Was Planned by Mercenaries," Associated Press, 29 June 2005.

88. <news.bbc.co.uk>, 29 June 2005.

89. Reuters, 30 July 2005.

90. Sean McCormack, press briefing, 29 July 2005, <www.state.gov>.

91. Agence France Presse, 14 July 2005.

92. See Arial Cohen, "Washington Grapples with Uzbekistan's Eviction Notice," 16 August 2005, <www.eurasianet.org>.

Index